AF540168

ATTITUDE TOWARDS SCIENCE

Attitude Towards Science

By
Dr. Gadde Bhuvaneswara Lakshmi
M.Sc., M.Ed., Ph.D.
Principal
Montessori Mahila College of Education
Vijayawada - 520 010
Andhra Pradesh, India

Editor
Dr. Digumarti Bhaskara Rao
M.Sc., M.A., M.A., M.Ed., Ph.D.
R.V.R. College of Education
Guntur - 522 006
Andhra Pradesh

Discovery Publishing House
New Delhi-110 002

First Published - 2000

Reprinted - 2018

ISBN: 978-81-7141-541-0

Attitude Towards Science

Published by:

DISCOVERY PUBLISHING HOUSE PVT. LTD.

4383/4B, Ansari Road, Darya Ganj

New Delhi-110 002 (India)

Phone: +91-11-23279245, 43596064-65

Fax: +91-11-23253475

E-mail: discoverypublishinghouse@gmail.com

sales@discoverypublishinggroup.com

web: www.discoverypublishinggroup.com

Printed at:

Infinity Imaging Systems

Delhi

Preface

Great scientific achievements and their use in promoting the well-being of mankind have made science more important than ever before. Because of its multi-dimensional nature, science has now become a compulsory part of general education and takes its place side by side with other subjects as an essential element of one's education.

There is a dire need to identify and develop positive attitude towards science subject. Now the time has come to increase own efforts to develop positive attitude towards science subject among in-service and preservice teachers and children. Hence, an investigation was carried out to study the attitude of the prospective science teachers towards science and this study was carried out to identify the level of attitude towards science and its psycho-social correlates. The prospective science teachers are having favourable attitude towards science, which is helpful in upgrading status of science instruction in coming years.

Thanks, with pleasure and sincerity, are extended to Prof. C.V. Raghavalu, Vice-chancellor, Nagarjuna University; Dr. V. Kofeswarama, Director and Correspondent, Montessori Mahila Educational Institutions; Prof. J.K. Dave and Dr. I.A. Vora, Sardar Patel University; Prof. P. Trimurthy and Dr. P. Syamala Trimurthy, Nagarjuna University; Dr. C. Sridevi, Monetessori Mahila College; Dr. G. Shyam Prasad, President, Lions Club; Sri Gadde Mangaiah, Secretary and Correspondent, RVR College of Education; Dr. K. Sadasiva Rao, President, RVR College of Education; Sri P. Lakshmana Rao, Bramhaial & Co., Chartered Accountants; and Sri Veeramechanani Venkataswara Rao, Secretary, Ravindra Bharathi Public School for their kind cooperation in every academic endeavour.

Bhuvaneswari
Bhaskara Rao

Contents

Introduction

Modern society is being influenced by the scientific environment and its application and science has become an integral part of our daily is very much which science and technology are racing is very much felt not only by Scientists. Economists , Administrators but also by the educationists. A citizen of modern India sees the countless manifestations of science all around him. There is no aspect of man's life today which has not been influenced by science in one way in the other. This is because we are living in an age of scientific culture. Science has shrunk the world and totally changed the human outlook. In fact, science now has an all pervading influence on every sphere of human activity. Further, modern science is no longer confined to the surface of this globe; its sphere of achievements reached beyond the earth.

In recent times , there has been rapid addition of knowledge to the world of science. Great advancements of science and technology and the use of scientific achievements in promoting well - being of mankind through their application in the fields of industry, communication, transport, engineering , agriculture, medicine have made science more important than ever before. Science has, in fact, radically transformed the material environment of the citizens of the modern . In addition to the immense and far-reaching material benefits of the science, as the Indian Education Commission puts it".... but even more profound is its contribution to culture. Science is liberating and encirching the mind and enlarging the human spirit. Its fundamental characters have turned out to be the possibility of unlimited growth. Every advance in science deepens our understanding of nature, but it also heightens the sense of ignorances. Nature is an inexhaustible knowable. Nothing comparable to scientific revolution in its impact on man's development and outlook since neolithic times." (Education Commission, 1964-66).

Science has to be explored further and further. So the exploring attitude, aptitude and ability have to be studied in the early stages of life. This can be greatly achieved with the help of teachers at all levels. Efforts are being made in this direction. It is also supported by Education Commission (1964).

"There is, of course, one thing about which we feel no doubt or hesitation, education which is science based and in coherence with Indian culture and values can alone provide the foundations, as also the instrument, for the nation's progress security and welfare (Education Commission, 1964-66).

Science is one of those human activities that man has created to gratify certain human needs desires. Curiosity has been the greatest motive power of scientific research. The search for truth has become the dominant motive in persuasion of science. As it is under persuasion since so many centuries it has attracted the attention of a very persisted group of people. Science is no longer confined to a few seriously devoted persons since the life in the present world invariably warrants to variable degrees of scientific facts and laws, science has now become every day science for everybody has become a part of general education. Science takes its place side by side with other subjects as an essential element of one's education. It affords a knowledge of certain facts and laws and an insight into methods and data peculiar to the domain of science. However, the inclusion of any subject in the curriculum should satisfy the intellectual, utilitarian, vocational, cultural, moral and aesthetic values. Besides these, the teaching of science imparts training in the scientific method and develops positive attitude towards science subject, scientific aptitude, which are very valuable and at the same time are transferable to other situations in the life of the learners. The qualities imbibed by the learner through learning science are of great value to the citizens living in the society.

The Scientific Policy Resolution of the Govt. of India (1958) states that "the dominating feature of the contemporary world is the intense cultivation to meet the country's requirement." Science has now become a compulsory subject in the school curriculum in every system of school education, right from elementary stage, because of its multifarious values gifted to the individual as well as to the society.

As Galileo has rightly said:

"the authority of a thousand is not worth the humble reasoning of a single individual".

Need and Importance of the Study

According to Education Commission "Science education must become an integral part of school education and ultimately study of science should become a part of all courses in the humanities and social sciences at the University stage." The Commission further says that "mingling of science and spirituality is of special significance for Indian education."

There is hardly any need to justify the place of science in a scheme of general education for school children. Science should help in reducing obstructionalism and all sorts of prejudices based on sex, caste, religion, language and region. By emphasizing a rational approach, science should help the development of a democratic, secular and socialistic state. There can be no doubt about the fact that in comparison to other subjects, the teaching of science has got some special significance, specially in secondary classes where a child lays the foundation for his future. In this age of science and technology where the progress of a country is estimated by its technological and scientific advancement, it is the most essential that more scientists must be produced in our country. And it is possible only if the teaching of science can be made more and more interesting, so that a good number of students may incline towards the study of science education.

According to a Bulletin of UNESCO (1971) "Teaching of science in some form or the other begins right from Class I in all the states and union territories. In classes I to V it is taught under different names, E.g.., Elementary Science, Nature Study, General Science, etc. Teaching of science as separate disciplines (Physics, Chemistry and Biology) was then introduced in a phased manner in Classes VI to VIII. Science gradually became a compulsory subject for all students up to Class VIII (World Survey of Education, 1971).

Joseph says "Science gives valuable mind-training. Science helps to train good citizens. We live in a world which is changing rapidly. The pupil needs some knowledge of science. If they are to understand the modern world, which depend so much on scientific discoveries, they need well disciplined minds, if they are to be useful citizens. Science helps to remove superstitutions and fear of the unknown. (Josephì, 1976).

So, science satisfies the urge to know, develops democratic

behaviour and also helps to develop scientific attitudes and critical thinking. It provides them sufficient knowledge for a successful living and also develops in them scientific outlook and positive attitudes.

H.N. Saunders describes the place of science in the curriculum as : "The inclusion of science in the curriculum is justified by the tremendous influence of science upon our modern civilization. The nature of the subject makes it worthy of a place for its own sake. Half-a-century ago science was struggling for a place in the scheme of education (Sanders , 1959).

In view of the above information the whole society accepts the importance of science. In order to recognize the importance of science positive attitude must be developed. It is the responsibility of each citizen to develop positive attitude towards science. Here the role of the teacher in inculcating positive attitude towards science is greater than any other individual. Before joining as teachers, teacher-trainees (prospective science teachers) they play a prominent role in inculcating positive attitude towards science subject, if they themselves have a positive attitude towards science.

Developing positive attitude towards science has been an exposed goal of most of curriculum development efforts since the late 1950s. It was hoped that increasing interest in science would result in increased science enrolment, which in turn would yield a larger science work force pool and a science literature public.

Having undergone the process of education every individual forms some kind of attitude towards science. These attitudes are likely to be permanent. Prospective teachers (B. Ed. trainees) are adults who have chosen teaching as their profession with a willingness to undergo a teacher training to perform various duties as teacher. It becomes easier if the prospective teachers possess the right attitude towards different subjects. Hence the secondary school science teachers are expected to possess positive attitude towards science which helps to improve themselves and to motivate the students in learning science and also in encouraging learning, training and research in the field of science.

Problem of the Present Study

There is a great need to identify and develop positive attitude towards science subject. Now the time has come to increase our efforts to develop positive attitude towards science subject among teachers, prospective teachers and school children. This is an immediate requirement of the present day. Reviewing the past literature the researcher felt the need to study the attitude of the prospective science teachers towards science and hence proposed to work with the following title:

"A study of the Attitude of Prospective Secondary School Science Teachers of Andhra Pradesh towards Science subject in the Context of some Psycho-Social Variables."

Operational Definitions of the Key Words

Scientists, psychologists, educationists, socialists define different words in different ways. The various definitions given by different experts are examined to select the appropriate meaning as the operational definitions of the terms used in the present research study. They are as follows :

1. Study
2. Science
3. Attitude
4. Attitude towards Science
5. Psychological variables
6. Scientific aptitude
7. Socio economic status
8. Personality

Study

The word study has different meanings. They are as follows:

According to Dictionary of Education study means :

1. Application of mind to a problem or subject, and
2. An investigation of particular subject.

According to the American Everyday Dictionary it means :

1. Application of mind to the acquisition of knowledge,
2. Deep thought, and
3. To examine or investigate carefully.

According to Comprehensive Desk Dictionary it means "some thing deserving attentive consideration".

According to Webster New Illustrated Dictionary it means :

1. To investigate closely, and
2. To scrutinize or earnestly contemplate.

The Reader's Digest Great Encyclopedia Dictionary defines the term study as :

1. Devotion of time and thought to acquisition of information, pursuit of some branch of knowledge, careful examination or observation of subject, question, etc.
2. Literary composition devoted to detailed consideration of a subject or problem or executed as exercise or experiment in style.
3. Careful sketch made for practice in technique or as a preliminary experiment or part of it, compositions designed to develop player's skill.
4. Make a study or take pain to investigate or acquire knowledge of subject. Assure, examine carefully, investigate, apply one-self to study, take pains to do deliberate, intentional effort.

Science

According to Dictionary of Science the meaning of the world Science is "the orderly arrangement of ascertained knowledge, including methods by which such knowledge is extended and the criteria by which its truth is tested. The older terms natural philosophy implied to the complementation of the natural process *per se* but modern science includes such study and control of nature as is or might be useful to mankind.

According to Dictionary of Education "Science of education is a systematized body of knowledge dealing with quantitative and objective aspects of learning process, employs instruction of precision in submitting hypothesis of education to the test of experience, frequently in the form of experimentation."

Albert Einstein said, "Science searches for relations, which are thought to exist independently of the searching individual."

Whitehead (1928), the famous philosopher defines Science as "an attempt to systematize our knowledge of the circumstances in which recognition occurs."

According to Frederic Fitzpatric, "Science is cumulative and endless series of empirical observations which result in the formation of concepts and theories with both the concepts and theories being subject to modification in the light of further empirical observations. Science is both a body of knowledge and a process of acquiring it."

Ames says, "Science is more than a compilation of facts. It is a method of thinking and working, a way of solving problems."

Conant (1948) defines that, "Science is an inter-connected series of concepts and theories. Science is a body of knowledge and the process of acquiring and refining knowledge."

Paul Hurd opined that "Facts themselves do not make a science. Science is not simply an abstraction from empirical data, but an intellectual occasion often suggested by data. It is the discerning of order among the data that makes the science. Science is an intellectual activity which arises from personal experience and takes place in the minds of men. It is simply a way of using human intelligence to achieve a better understanding of nature and nature's laws."

B.F. Skinner, a great psychologist, defined Science as "First of all, Science is a set of attitudes. It is a disposition to deal with facts rather than with what some one has said about them."

Green, A.W. says "Science is a way of investigation".

In the words of Poincare, "Science is built of facts as a house is built of stones, but an accumulation of facts is no more a science than a heap of stones".

According to Weinerg and Shabat "Science is certain way of looking at the world".

The Columbia Encyclopedia defined science as "..... accumulated and systematized learning, in general usage, restricted to natural phenomenon. The progress of science is marked not only by an accumulation of facts, but by the emergence of scientific method and of the scientific attitude."

For the present research work the definition given by Fredric Fitpatric is accepted by the researcher.

Attitude

The term attitude, like most abstract terms in English language, has more than one meaning. Herbert Spencer was one of the earliest psychologists to employ this term. Derived from the Latin word "Aptus" it has on one had the significance of fitness or connotes a subjective or mental state of preparation for action. On other hand, an attitude is an effective by product of an individual's experience and has its base in inner urges, acquired habits and environmental influences by which an individual is surrounded. In other words, the attitude is a result of personal desires and group stimulation. It is the part of individual's personality. But, an individual will be affected by the attitude and behaviour of the groups with which he is associated.

The attitude is a concept of belief. One does or does not favour a particular object. One accepts some path or rejects it. All these beliefs, favourableness and acceptance are the expressions of an attitude.

Fowler and Fowler (1968) give the meaning of attitude as a "Behaviour of conduct regarding some matters."

Atkinson (1970) defines Attitude as "reactions that may or may not reflect the individual's observations of his own behaviour. Attitudes are often called unspoken opinion.

Hariman (1950) states that "An attitude is defined as a mental set to respond to a situation with a proper reaction where as sets may be temporary matters, attitudes are more or less stable."

According to Walter (1950) "an attitude means mental or neural state of readiness organized through experience, expecting a directive or dynamic influence upon the individual's response to all objects and situations with which it is treated."

Thurstone and Chave (1929) define attitude as "The sum total of man's inclination and feelings, prejudices or biases, Preconceived notions, ides, fears, threats and convictions about any specific topic.

According to Woodworth (1994) "An attitude is a set of dispositions (readiness, inclination, tendency) to act towards an object according to its characteristics so far as we are acquainted with them.

Stephens (1951) explains that "An attitude means something that is learnt without any intention whatever it is.

David Krech (1962) defines that "An attitude is an enduring system of positive or negative evaluations, emotional feeling, and action tendencies with respect to a social object."

According to Charles Skinner (1966) "An attitude is defined as a Generalized disposition towards a group of people and it is promotionally tended"

Norman Marries (1964) presents that "Attitude are associated with likes and consequently have an emotional content."

Brown (1965) has defined attitude as "an acquired and relatively fixed tendency to react in a given way in relation to other persons or thing.

Glimer (1970) writes that "An attitude is a tendency to respond positively or negatively to other people, to decisions, to institutions, and to organisations."

Guilford (1959) says that "An attitude is a disposition a person has to favour or not to favour a type of social object or social action."

John (1971) defines, attitude as an "implicit drive producing a response considered socially significant in the individual's society."

Edwards (1957) defines attitude as " a degree of positive or negative affect associated with some psychological object.

According to Thordike and Hagen (1957). "An attitude means a feeling of favourableness and unfavourbleness towards some groups, institutions or propositions.

Attitude Towards Science Subject

An attitude is an emotional reaction towards a person or object. It is a personal response to a person or object developed through experiences, which can be characterised as a favourable or unfavourable one. The use of science as the object or the stimulus of these feelings delineates that a set of attitudes known as attitude towards science.

It is defined as an opinion or position taken with respect to a psychological object in the field of science. (Richard W. Moore 1970).

According to International Encyclopedia of Education "Science attitudes are positive or negative feelings that an individual holds about science subject."

For the present study the science attitude, therefore, operationally be defined as a generalized attitude towards the universe of science content and being measured in terms of its favourableness or unfavorableness.

Psycho-Social Variables

An individual's learning to think, feel and behave in an adult way is the function of socialization. Age, sex, area, attitudes, aptitudes and other physical make-up and mental potentialities have an immense impact on it. This ultimately results into a set of reaction-habits which is known as a personality trait. Hence the researcher viewed that these psycho-socio-economic variables may have some effect on the development of attitude towards science subject. Some human behaviours have been classified and have been named by exponents of different schools of psychology. The researcher has accepted the trait theory of personality and selected carefully a few apparently related traits with the attitudes concept.

Scientific Aptitude

Though the term aptitude is differently defined it includes certain essentials such a present ability, role of training, case of acquiring proficiency, interest in activity, and so on.

In the Dictionary of Education aptitude is defined as a "Pronounced innate capacity for or ability in a given line of endeavour such as a particular art, school subject or vocation. Thus, in the definition, an aptitude refers to an individual's internal capacities or potentialities which are indicative of some special abilities."

According to English and English (1958) it may be regarded as "the capacity to acquire proficiency with a given amount of training.

Aptitude in Great Illustrated Dictionary is defined as "a natural talent, skill or ability, quickness in learning and understanding.

Here in the above definitions, it has been emphasized that an aptitude refers to the capacity of an individual to be skilled in some work receiving formal or informal training.

Freeman (1965) has defined an aptitude as a "Combination of characteristics indicative of an individual's capacity to acquire (with training) some specific knowledge, skill, set of organized responses such as the ability to speak a language, to become a musician, to do a mechanical work." Freeman has also pointed out that the aptitude is different from skill and proficiency. He has further stated that "... when we speak of an individual's aptitude for a given type of activity we mean the capacity to acquire proficiency under as revealed by his performance on selected tests that have predictive value." In other words, the most important factor of an aptitude is the capacity to acquire proficiency. On the other hand if an individual has no aptitudes for a particular type of task, he will not be skilled or proficient in the task in spite of the training given to him. These aptitudes refer to an individual's internal capacity to acquire proficiency in a given area of human endeavour.

The aptitude is a capacity in any given skill or field of knowledge, on the basis of which a prediction may be made regarding the amount of improvement which further training might effect.

Many agree on the point that the aptitudes are innate. Nevertheless it is also realised that aptitudes are influenced by the environment in which the individual lives. In other words, though aptitudes are innate and mostly governed by hereditary factors, yet environmental factors play an important role. As a matter of fact, the biological and culture factors are involved in all psychological activities of an individual.

The aptitudes are fairly constant for a period of time variations occur within the framework of environmental factors as it is generally believed that aptitude is like intelligent quotient.

But, according to Wringtstone, *et al.* (1956) "While the evidence is confliciting, the trend seems to be in the direction of assuming that aptitudes are some what variables and are affected within limits by the educational and environmental influences."

Educators had first considered aptitude as mystery, i.e. a function of a single general trait or characteristic. But, factor analytic technique indicates that an aptitude need not necessarily be the function of a single general trait.

Kelly identified verbal, numerical, spatial, motor, musical, social and mechanical; and verbal influency, number, memory, spatial, reasoning, deduction and induction abilities which were indicative of pherastic aptitudes."

Dressel (1963) defines that "Scientific aptitude is a potentiality for future accomplishment in science without regard to past training and achievement.

Super states that "Scientific aptitude is presumably largely an intellectual matter, and it seems that a battery of tests for the selection of promising scientists will stress such factors as reasoning, spatial visualisation, number ability, scientific vocabulary and mechanical comprehension are too pure aptitudes which should also be significant.

Socio Economic Status

Socio economic status is defined as social prestige enjoyed by means of education, occupation and economic status. According to Good (1945), SES is "the level of indicative of both the social and economic achievement of an individual or group.

Personality

According to Good (1945) Personality is "the total psychological and social reaction of an individual; the synthesis of his subjective, emotional and mental life, his behaviour, and his reactions to the environment; the unique or individual traits of a person are connoted to a lesser degree by a personality than by the terms of character.

Morton Prince defined personality as "the sum total of all the biological innate dispositions, impulses, tendencies, appetites and instincts of the individual and the dispositions and the tendencies acquired by experience."

William Healy defines it as "an integrated system of habitual adjustment to the environment, particularly to the social environment."

Burhum says that "Personality is a totality, not in the sense of a mere summation but as a synthesis what characterises personality, above all is interaction or wholeness."

Murphy writes that "Personality is not the sum or even the interaction of separate traits but it is a unitary mode of adjustment in relating to which search specific activity or interest, no matter, how trivial must be seen."

Wright, *et. al.* (1970) defines personality as "The relatively stable and enduring aspects of the individual which distinguish him from other people at the same time form the basis of our predictions concerning his future behaviour."

Allport also regarded personality as of a dynamic nature and as an integrated whole with distinct and unique role in social or environmental adjustment. He writes, "personality is the dynamic organisation wit in the psycho-physical system that determines his unique adjustment to his environment."

Traxler defines Personality from the point of view of measurement of personality traits. In his words ".... personality will be defined as the sum total of an individual's behaviour in social situations."

Objectives of the Study

The main objectives of the present study are to analyse the extent to which select socio-economic background and personality variables influence the attitudes of prospective secondary school science teachers toward science; to portrays the patterns of interaction among various sets of attitudional variables and to draw inferences about the dominant sources of influence on attitude towards science of the respondents. The following are the objective of the present study:

1. To study the attitude of prospective science teachers towards science subject.
2. To study the scientific aptitude of prospective science teachers.
3. To study the socio economic status of prospective science teachers.
4. To study self-sufficiency vs. dependency level of prospective science teachers.
5. To study dominance vs. submissiveness level of prospective science teachers.
6. To study introversion vs. extroversion level of prospective science teachers.
7. To study the emotional stability level of prospective science teachers.
8. To study the sex-wise attitude of prospective science teachers towards science subject.
9. To study the methodology-wise attitude of prospective science teachers towards science subject.
10. To study the area-wise attitude of prospective science teachers towards science subject.
11. To study the main effect of sex on attitude towards science subject.
12. To study the main effect of methods of teaching on attitude towards science subject.
13. To study the main effect of area on attitude towards science subject.
14. To study the main effect of scientific aptitude on attitude towards science subject.
15. To study the main effect of SES on attitude towards science subject.
16. To study the main effect of self sufficiency vs. dependency personality trait on attitude towards science subject.
17. To study the main effect of dominance vs. submissiveness personality trait on attitude towards science subject.
18. To study the main effect of introversion vs. extroversion personality trait on attitude towards science subject.
19. To study the main effect of emotional stability personality trait on attitude towards science subject.
20. To study the interaction effect between sex and methods of teaching on attitude towards science subject.
21. To study the interaction effect between sex and scientific aptitude on attitude towards science subject.

22. To study the interaction effect between sex and SES on attitude towards science subject.
23. To study the interaction effect between sex and self sufficiency vs. dependency on attitude towards science subject.
24. To study the interaction effect between sex and dominance vs. submissiveness on attitude towards science subject.
25. To study the interaction effect between sex and emotional stability on attitude towards science subject.
26. To study the interaction effect between methods of teaching and are on attitude towards science subject.
27. To study the interaction effect between methods of teaching and scientific aptitude on attitude towards science subject.
28. To study the interaction effect between methods of teaching and SES on attitude towards science subject.
29. To study the interaction effect between methods of teaching and self sufficiency vs. dependency on attitude towards science subject.
30. To study the interaction effect between methods of teaching and dominance vs. submissiveness on attitude towards science subject.
31. To study the interaction effect between methods of teaching and introversion vs. extroversion on attitude towards science subject.
32. To study the interaction effect between methods of teaching and emotional stability on attitude towards science subject.
33. To study the interaction effect among sex, methods of teaching and area on attitude towards science subject.
34. To study the interaction effect among sex, methods of teaching and scientific aptitude on attitude towards science subject.
35. To study the interaction effect among sex, methods of teaching and SES on attitude towards science subject.
36. To study the interaction effect among sex, methods of teaching and self sufficiency vs. dependency on attitude towards science subject.
37. To study the interaction effect among sex, methods of teaching and dominance vs. submissiveness on attitude towards science subject.
38. To study the interaction effect among sex, methods of

teaching and introversion vs. extroversion on attitude towards science subject.

39. To study the interaction effect among sex, methods of teaching and emotional stability on attitude towards sceince subject.

Hypotheses of the study

Null hypotheses had been formulated and tested during the course of the study. Sex and methods of teaching are taken as common independent variables in all the studies. Therefore, they are seen to be running common in all the studies and only the third independent variable keeps on changing in order to study the effect of dependent variable attitude towards science subject. The Null hypotheses taking area as the third independent variable are presented below:

1. There is no significant main effect of sex on attitude of prospective teachers towards science subject.
2. There is no significant main effect of methods of teaching on attitude of prospective science teachers.
3. There is no significant main effect of area on attitude of prospective science teachers towards science subject.
4. There is no significant interaction effect between sex and methods of teaching on attitude of prospective science teachers towards science subject.
5. There is no significant interaction effect between sex and area on attitude of prospective science teachers towards science subject.
6. There is no significant interaction effect between methods of teaching and area on attitude towards science subject.
7. There is no significant interaction effect among sex, methods of teaching and area on attitude towards science subject.

The same pattern and the number of hypotheses had been followed to formulate the hypotheses for the third changing independent variables, namely scientific aptitude, SES, self sufficiency vs. dependency, dominance vs. submissiveness, introversion vs. extroversion and emotional stability. The framed hypotheses for each study are presented in detail in chapter VI.

Limitations of the Present study

The present study has certain limitations. They are as follows :

1. The study is limited to the five colleges of education in Krishna and Guntur Districts of A.P.
2. The sample consists of only prospective science teachers.
3. The sample comprises of prospective science teachers coming from both English and Telugu (regional language) media.
4. The researcher has selected only self-sufficiency vs. dependency, dominance vs. submissiveness, introversion vs. extroversion and emotional stability as personality traits to stud the psychological aspects of prospective science teachers.
5. The answer given by the student teachers assumed to be true and reliable.

The scheme of Chapterization

A brief description of the chapters to follow is given here:

Chapter - I, Introduction

In this chapter introduction, need for the study, objectives, hypotheses and limitations of the study along with the title and its operational definitions are presented.

Chapter - II, Theoretical Perspective

This chapter enumerates the theoretical concept of attitude the various views given by psychologists, educationists, etc. and are presented along with its importance the need to measure the attitude and the favouring factors for developing attitude towards science subject.

Chapter - III, Review of the past literature

It gives a short review of the past studies. This chapter presents a few studies on science, attitude towards science subject, scientific attitude and scientific aptitude. It contains mainly significant contributions made in different places. It helps the researcher in formulating the hypotheses, planning the research design and sample; identifying the statistical techniques and arriving at conclusions.

Chapter - IV, Planning and Procedure

This chapter deals with the research design planning and selection of research tools; variables and the procedure adopted for the selection of the sample and statistical techniques.

Chapter - V, Data Collection and Presentation

This chapter deals with the sampling techniques, characteristics of the sample to conduct the study.

Chapter - VI, Analysis and Interpretation

The data collected for the study is tabulated and analysed with the help of computer. The statistical tests include "F" test, 2x2x2 factorial design, and analysis of variance.

Chapter - VII, Summary, Findings and Suggestions

This chapter deals with a brief resume of the earlier chapters. It also includes the researcher's observations and experiences in conducting the study. The conclusions will be reported. Finally, suggestions for further studies in this field are to be suffixed.

Thus this thesis contains the detailed description of all essential steps taken to study, the attitude of prospective secondary school science teachers towards science subject along with its effective correlates. It is also embedded with tables. Reported bibliography and appendices at the end of the report will give a clear picture of the books referred and the tools used.

2

Theoretical Perspective

Introduction

This chapter enumerates the theoretical concept of attitudes and the various views given by psychologists, educationists, etc. and are presented along with its importance, the need to measure the attitude and the favouring factors for developing attitude towards science subject.

Concept of Attitudes

The concept of attitudes is an old one in psychology, and we tend to associate it more directly with the area of social psychology. It was an important concept in general psychology in Germany at the time of the twentieth century. It was first used in America by Franklin H. Giddings, the Sociologist, and was introduced into Social Psychology by William I. Thomas. The first American psychologist to use the concept in a general text book was Howard C. Warren, in his "Human Psychology". Allport referred Attitude to as "the most distinctive and indispensable concept in contemporary American social Psychology". Thurstone boldly asserted that Attitude can be measured. The concept of attitudes no doubt, gained more general acceptance by American psychologists as a result of the influence of Giddings and Thomas, both of whom were professional sociologists.

The concept of attitudes has several characteristics that differentiate it from other concepts referring to internal states of the individual. Sherif and Sherif (1968) state that:

1. Attitudes are innate. They belong to that domain of human motivation variously studied under the labels of 'social

drives,' 'social needs', 'social orientation', and the like. It is assumed that the appearance of an attitude is dependent on learning.

2. Attitudes are not temporary states but are more or less enduring once they are formed. Of course, attitudes do change; but formed they acquire a regulatory function such that, within limits, they are not subject to change with the ups and downs of hameostatic functioning of the organism or with every first - noticeable variation in stimulus conditions.
3. Attitudes always imply a relationship between the person and objects. In other words, attitudes are not self-generated psychologically. They are formed or learned in relation to identifiable referents, whether these be persons, groups, institutions, objects, values, social issues or ideologies.
4. The relationship between person and object is not neutral but has motivational - affective properties. These properties derive from the context of highly significant social interaction in which many attitudes are formed, from the fact that the objects are not neutral for the participants and from the fact that self, as it develops, acquires positive value for the person. Therefore, the linkage between self and the social environment is seldom neutral.
5. The subject-object relationship is accomplished through the formation of categories both differentiating between the person's positive or negative relation to objects in various categories. The referent of an attitude constitutes a set that may range, theoretically, from one to the large number of objects. However, in actuality the formation of a positive or negative stand towards one object usually implies differential attachment to other in the same domain.

Aggarwal (1964) summarizes the concept of Attitudes through following characteristics:

1. There is no limited range of attitudes, our likes, dislikes, food we take, everything is an aspect of attitude.
2. It is a position towards the objects, either for or against.
3. There are individual differences in attitudes.
4. They are the bases of behaviour as they lead to strike, war, voting, etc.

5. They may be overt or covert.
6. They are integrated into an organised system.
7. They are acquired and not inborn.
8. Attitude towards on object is not necessarily based on its utility. For example, attitude towards food is not based on its nutritional value.
9. They differ from culture to culture.
10. They are more or less lasting but they can be modified.
11. They always imply a subject-object relationship.
12. Reference of an attitude may be one item or a number of items. For example, in case of fighting against a nation, most of its members are enemies.

Gardon W. Allport (1967) selected some representative characteristics of attitude which are listed below :

1. It is a readiness for attention or action of a definite sort (Baldwin - 1901 - 1905).
2. Attitudes are literally mental postures, guides for conduct to which each new experience is referred to before response is made.
3. An attitude is a complex of feelings, desires, fears, convictions, prejudices or other tendencies that have given a set or readiness to act to a person because of varied experiences (Chave - 1928).
4. An attitude is a mental disposition of the individual to act for or against a definite object (Broba - 1933).
5. An attitude denotes the general set of the organism as a whole towards an object or situation which calls for adjustment (Lundberg - 1920)
6. Attitudes are modes of emotional regard for object and motor "set" or slight tentative reaction towards them (Ower - 1929).
7. An attitude is more or less permanently enduring state of readiness of mental organization which predisposes an individual to react in a characteristic way to any object or situation with which it is related.

Importance of Attitudes

The importance of attitudes is very great. They permeate our whole life and our self-concept is essentially the sum total of attitudes by which we live. They make a great difference in almost everyone's life. They offer great possibilities for successful achievement as well as failure in life. Efficiency results when a person is impelled by his attitude to start, continue, and compete a project rather than to avoid an unpleasant task.

The attitude of an individual towards his work affects his worthwhileness in the activity. The businessman depends upon the favourable attitude of his customers towards his product and services to keep his business going. The politician must have favourable attitudes towards his personality, ability and political behaviour in order to count on his re-election. The hard-working person has favourable attitudes towards all those experiences and situations in which hard work is necessary. The successful teacher has favourable attitudes towards his students, his friends, his subjects and his principal. The person who considers himself very clever tries to be clever in all situations.

Attitudes are considered as important motivators of behaviour and affect all human values. Crow and Crow (1973) writes that:

"His attitude towards others determines his social values. If the individual can learn to forget self and to be of service to those who need help, he has achieved personality characteristics that are essential to the gaining of appreciation from others. If he does not feel superior to the work that he is doing or to the people with whom he is associated, he is likely to succeed in his work in his social relationship".

There are, indeed, very few acts or decisions in everyday affairs that do not somehow take account of the way in which attitudes may be affected. Therefore, the cultivation of attitude towards these values and ideas which society cherishes and appreciates is the best way of promoting behaviour consistent with the accepted codes and morals of the social order.

From the point of view of learning, attitudes are important in as much as they facilitate further learning and thus contain within themselves the course of further motivation. Attitude must be aroused and developed for a child. Every school cannot escape from its responsibility of organizing a deliberate plans and programmes of influencing positive attitudes in the child.

The child should not be permitted to do completely as he wishes. He should be stimulated towards desirable activity through the arousal of interest in worthwhile projects. Constructive and objective attitudes during childhood serve well during adolescence. The attitude of the teacher, of the parent, or of a group leader is important. Each should display the kind of objective but understanding attitude that will be a good attitude for the child to imitate.

Education of the child, therefore, must include the development or right attitudes as well as the acquisition of behaviour habits that are socially desirable. Not only some rules and regulations concerning good conduct and effective playing habits be taught, but they should be understood and appreciated in the light of their values to the individual and society. Counts (1952) states the importance of values in these words :

"The essence of any civilization is found in its values - in its performances, its moral commitments, its aesthetic judgements, its deepest loyalties, its conception of the good life, its standard of excellence, its nature of success, it teachings regarding the things for which and by which men should live, if need be, die. The issue at stake in the coming years is nothing less than the birth, the death, and the survival of values."

Promoting favourable attitudes, therefore, in an individual is an asset both to him and to society. Promoting favourable attitude towards Science Education is to encourage him to take part in Science Education programmes still further. The individual should be aided in making deliberate choice of behaviour in harmony with his own and society's betterment. He should strive to create favourable attitudes and eliminate unfavourable ones.

Measurement of Attitudes

To use the concept of attitudes in understanding and predicting action, one needs reliable and valid measurement. The measurement of attitudes, like the measurement of all psychological determinants is necessarily indirect. Attitude can be measured only on the basis of inference drawn from the responses of the individual towards the object, his overt actions and his verbal statements of beliefs, feelings and dispositions to act with respect to the object. Several methods have been employed to measure attitudes, they are as follows :

Method of Direct Questioning

In this method, the individual is asked directly how he feels about the object. By means of direct questioning one might be able to classify individuals into three groups, those with favourable attitudes, and those who say that they are doubtful or undecided about their attitudes towards the object. This technique may be employed as a schedule or questionnaire of the open or closed form. It may be employed as the interview process in which the respondent express his opinion only.

Method of Direct Observation of Behaviour

This method is to observe the behaviour of individuals with respect to a psychological object. There are limitations to this approach. The researcher interested in the attitudes of large number of individuals towards the object may not have the opportunity to observe in detail the behaviour of all the individuals in whom he is interested. In many cases an individual may conceal his real feeling and express socially acceptable opinions. Individuals are all aware of situations in which they have acted contrary to the way in which they felt because of various reasons. If a politician kisses babies in public, his behaviour may not be a true expression of affection towards infants. Attitudes, as factors influencing or determining behaviours may be one of many such, and not necessarily the most prepotent factors. If one expects to predict behaviour from feelings or attitudes, then those other factors must be taken into account. And similarly, if one expects to infer attitudes or feelings from direct observations of behaviour, one must always consider the possibility that our inference may be incorrect simply because the behaviour may be determined by factors other than the individual's feelings.

Attitude Scales

Of all the methods for the measurement of attitudes, by far the most widely used and the most carefully designed and tested is the attitude scale, which typically yields a total score indicating the direction and intensity of an individual's attitude towards the object. An attitude scale consists of a set of statements or items to which the person responds. Each of the statements is assigned with a set of numerical values. The pattern of an individuals's responses provides a way of inference, something about his attitude.

The development of attitude scale has involved several techniques. Each has its own merits and demerits. Two of these techniques have been used exensively in attitude or opinion research, and warrant a brief description. They are:

1. Bogardus Social Distance Scale.
2. Thurston's Method of Equal-appearing Intervals.
3. Likert's Method of Summated Ratings.

1. The Bogardus Social Distance Scale

Bogardus (1924) devised a series of statements representing different degrees of social intimancy for varying social groups. Subjects (sample) indicate the degree of relationship of which they would admit members of a given group. This particular test in used in assessing attitudes relating to racial or ethnic prejudice.

2. Thurston's Method of Equal-Appearing Intervals

Thurston's Method of attitude assessment is known as the Thurston Technique of scale values or the Method of Equal-Appearing Intervals. The first step in constructing the Thurston type scale is to collect the statements that express various points of view towards the particular object. Those statements are edited and then submitted to panel of judges and each one of them arranges the statements in eleven groups, ranging from the most favourableness to the most unfavourableness is position. This sorting by each judge yields a composite position of each of the items. The median of the judged locations for a statement, is its scale value. Statements that are judged to be ambiguous or irrelevant to the continuum are eliminated.

Before inclusion in the final scale, each question is analysed for consistency with the general attitudes found by the total score. For example, on a scale to determine attitudes towards social value, if it is found that many persons having an unfavourable attitude check a statement that is apparently favourable, then that item is considered irrelevant and is discarded. Statements having approximately the same values in the scale should show high consistency in degree of endorsement by each subject. This is essentially a simple method of item analysis. Ambiguity of an item is determined by the spread of range of judges rating in the original eleven point scale, given in terms of Q (quartile deviation). If an item's Q is high, it is eliminated. For items those are retained, each is given its median scale value, between one and eleven as established by the penal.

The list of statements, twenty or twenty two, is then given to the subjects, who are asked to check the statements with which they are in agreement. The median value of the statements that they check establishes their score, or quantifies their opinion. The person who has the large score is more favourably inclined towards the attitude object than the person with a lower scale.

3. Likert's Method of Summated Ratings

The Likert type scale presents a number of positive and negative statements regarding the attitude object. In responding to the item on this scale, the subjects indicate whether they strongly agree, undecided, disagree or strongly disagree with each statement. The numerical value assigned to each response depends on the degree of agreement or disagreement with individual statement. The score of a person is determined by means of a summing of the values assigned to individual responses. For example, one may score a Likert type scale by assigning a value of five points to each response indicating strong agreement with favourable statements, a value of four for agreement with these statements, three for being undecided, two for disagreement, and one for strong disagreement. For unfavourable statements one reverses the scoring procedure, since disagreement with an unfavourable statement is assumed to be psychologically equivalent to agreement with a favourable statement.

To construct a Likert-type scale, the following steps are usually taken :

1. Collect a large number of favourable and unfavourable statements regarding the attitude object.
2. Select from these approximately equal number of favourable and unfavourable statements.
3. Administer these items to a number of individuals, asking them to indicate that opinions regarding each statement by determining whether they strongly agree, undecided, disagree or strongly disagree with each statement.
4. Compute the score of each individual using the scoring procedure discussed previously.
5. Carry out the item analysis to select those times that yield the best discrimination. Though item analysis one finds the correlation between the subjects' total scores and their response to each item.

The Likert scale uses items worded for or against the position, with five point rating response indicating the strength of the respondent's approval or disapproval of the statement. The check or tick on the five point rating responses are weighted simply 1 to 5. Items are summated over the total number of items and a summative score obtained. This procedure makes the Likert Method very much like on ordinary test.

Eycnck and Crown (1949) have proposed a combination of the two methods - Thrston's and Likert's - by giving the statements, the Thurston scale value and response, the Likert weight, Both Thurston and Likert scales are specific as to the issue or object the attitude towards which is measured.

Attitudes Towards Science

An attitude is an emotional reaction towards a person or thing. It is a personal response to an object, developed through experience which can be characterised as favourable or unfavourable. The use of science as the object or stimulus of these feelings delineates that set of attitudes known as 'attitudes towards science'.

Developing positive attitudes towards science has been an exposed goal of most of the curriculum development efforts since the last 1950s (Welch 1979). It was hoped that increasing interest in science would result in increased science enrolment which in turn would yield a larger science work force pool and a science literate public. The increased attention to the effective outcomes of science has also resulted in a proliferation of attitude research studies, more measuring techniques, and several attempts to measure attitude towards science on an international scale.

Recent reviews of research on science attitudes also reflect the burgeoning work in this area. Sufficient studies now exist to enable researchers to conduct quantity syntheses of research results. These integrative studies, called meta-analysis have been done for science attitudes and provide additional understanding of the accomplishments and problems in this area.

Status of Attitude Towards Science

There is a wide spread belief among scientists and science educators that attitudes towards science are negative than is desired. Declining enrolment, and personal experiences have created a generally discouraging situation. According to International Encyclopedia of Education, teachers and principals report their belief that the public's image towards science has declined in recent years.

Favouring Factors for Developing Attitudes Towards Science

In spite of the apparent logical connection between science attitudes and science achievements, the research results suggest a very modest positive relationship. A consistent positive relationship has been noted between gender and attitudes. Males take more science course and show more interest, especially in the physical sciences.

Several researches have pointed out that interest in science develops early in life (between the ages of 8 and 13) and call for increased attention to the science experiences of that age group. At that age, many children express positive attitudes towards science but this attitude decreases over time. Those that do tend to choose science course and careers appear to have certain personality traits which are related to positive science attitudes.

One consistent set of attitude correlates is other measures of science attitudes. Another group of endogenous variables which has been correlated with student attitudes are the home background variables. Included here are such things as geographic location, parents' education, father's occupation, and science materials in the home. Geographic location (e.g. urban, suburban, or rural) as well as native country are related to science attitudes. Socio economic status and science opportunities in the home are correlated moderately with science interest and science carrier choice. The direct influence of the home and background factors is difficult to assess because they interest with each other. Parents attitude toward science seems important but it in turn is related to parents' education, home opportunity, college choice and so on.

Several researchers have turned to those variables under the potential control of the schools in their attempts to discover the means by which attitudes towards science could be enhanced. Although some important relationships, have been discovered, much remains to be done in this area.

In general, there are low, but positive, relationships between teaching and behaviour, the science curriculum, and student attitudes. Curriculum effects may account for perhaps 5-10 percent of student variance in attitude (and achievement) (Ormerod and Duckworth 1975, Welch 1979), but other factors, especially student and teacher variables, appear to be more influential.

The teacher is thought to play an important role in the development or hindrance of student attitude. Although much more work has been done on student achievement than on student attitudes, attributes such as enthusiasm, respect of students and personality traits have been shown to influence student attitudes in science as well as in other subjects.

The influence of students peers has been the subject of some recent investigations and appears to provide some explanations of attitude development. The social learning environment, peer pressure, and nature of student interactions seems to be related to the attitudes that students have towards science and their science classes. The exact nature of these relationships, is still not clear but the social experiences as a student has in a class with his or her classmates, and more importantly with the teacher, are powerful influences on the attitudes a student carries away from that class.

There are marked differences in the classroom climate across subjects areas, teachers, age groups, and even from year to year. Just how these factors influence the development of attitudes towards science appears to be an important area of investigation. Equally important is the role that the teacher plays in shaping the classroom climate and its influence on fostering positive attitudes.

According to Internal encyclopedia Vol VII, it is summarised that attitudes towards science is a growing area for research, but attitudes are difficult to measure effectively, are perceived as generally low, and seem to reflect a declining image of science. There is a low positive correlation between since achievement and attitudes, and in addition, males generally express more positive attitudes than females. Attitudes decline across age levels, and exposure to science experience often produces negative attitude changes. Low curriculum effects and special influences have been found but some potential for enhancing science attitudes has been found with classroom climate measures and teacher behaviour.

3

Review of Related Literature

Introduction

"Every serious piece of research includes a review of related research. But, where do the original ideas and concepts come from? And how can they be linked to form hypothesis? To some extent they come out of the researcher's head, but to a large extent they come from the collective body of prior work referred to as the literature". - Bruce W. Tuckman

A researcher before taking up any research, primarily needs to study the past literature available in the concerned field. Awareness of the past literature enlightens the researcher with the sources that are available in the field, their worthiness and unability.

Good, Barr and Scates (1941) analysed the purpose of research review as 'To select suitable research method to the problem; to locate the date useful in the interpretation of results and to provide ideas, theories, explanations or hypotheses valuable in formulations the problem'.

In searching related literature, the research should note certain important elements. They include....

1. Reports of closely related studies.
2. Design of the study including procedures employed and data gathering instruments used.
3. Population that were sampled and sampling methods employed.
4. Variables that were defined.
5. Extraneous variables that could have affected the findings,
6. Faults that could have been avoided, and
7. Recommendations for further research.

Capitalizing on the reviews of expert researchers can be fruitful in providing helpful ideas and suggestions. While review articles that summarise related studies are useful, they do not provide a satisfactory substitute for an independent work. But it is valuable guide, to define problems, to recognize its significance, to suggest promising data gathering devices, to study design and sources of data for effective analysis and to arrive at fruitful conclusions.

The search for related literature is necessary for a good research work. Hence this chapter, review of related literature, is meant for the study of objectives that lead to the inclusion of positive attitude towards science subject, scientific aptitude, SES and personality of the individual. It is also meant for the study of the research works related to attitude towards science subject, scientific aptitude, SES and personality and the inter-relationship among these factors.

Education Commission (1964-66) states that "science education must become an integral part of school education and ultimately some study of science should become a part of all courses in the humanities and social sciences.... The quality of science teaching is to be developed considerably so as to achieve its proper objectives and purposes; viz., to understand basic principles; to develop problem solving; analytical skills and ability; to apply them to the problem of material environments and social living besides promoting the spirit of enquiry and experimentation. Science strengthens commitments of man to free enquity and research for truth, it even helps to lessen ideological tensions."

Although it is largely occupied with the understanding of nature at present, its development is tending more and more to help man to understand himself and his place in the world. In such developments, the Commission observes that the pursuit of mere material affluence and power would be subordinated to that of higher values and the fulfilment of the individual. The concept of mingling of science and spirituality is of special significance in Indian education.

It is commonly felt that a child's education cannot be complete unless he has some knowledge of science irrespective of the field of study he wishes to pursue in latter life. Today the great advances in science rendered it absolutely necessary that a fundamental knowledge of science should be the *Sine Qua non* of any person who was educated and who wished to lead a life which combined is itself something of scientific aspects of existence.

"Since can justify its place in the curriculum only when it reduces important changes in young pupils. Change in their ways of thinking, in their habits of action and in the values they assign to what they have and what they do. (Hurd, 1954).

Research in science Education

Science education occupies a very prominent place in curriculum, both at school and university stages of education in India. Continuous advances in scientific and technological research has led to the growth and greater application of science incontemporary society. Accordingly science becomes a priority area in education, both at a compulsory education level as well as the level of specialization. Science education is supposed to perform a two fold task. The prime objective in individualistic perspective, is the cultivation of scientific temper which includes a spirit of enquiry, disposition to reason logically and disassionately, a habit of judging beliefs and opinions on available evidence, readiness to reject unfounded theories and principles to encourage to admit facts howsoever, unsetting or disagreeable they might be, and finally recognizing the limits of reasoning power itself. It is also expected of science education that would give individuals a firm grasp of the concepts and processes of science and impart to them the ability to use scientific method of problem solving techniques of observations and eperimentation in handling problem comprehension of life. At the societal level one of the major objectives of science education is to equip individuals to participate in the creation of a society which is free from poverty, hunger, disease and evils such as violence, exploitation, oppression, etc.

Researches in science education have to be reviewed in the context of these aims and objectives. In the world of today where knowledge is being multiplied exponentially, science education will not be able to justify itself remaining merely contented with the objective of imparting a certain quantum of scientific knowledge however large be the quantum. Since the rate at which knowledge in science today gets obsolete is very high compound to that in the forties or fifties, it is essential that the emphasis of science education should be on the development of abilities and dispositions of mind rather than merely the transfer of dead subject matter. This analysis might find acceptance among educationists and researchers in education but it is not enough. Research in science education should be urgently addressed to the problem of developing positive attitude towards science subject and scientific attitude and scientific aptitude in the education. Intensive studies will have to be directed towards these fundamental aspects of science education.

What are the elements of positive attitude towards sceince? How can it be assured accurately? Which strategies are most appropriate to inculcate the spirit of science in students?

What steps should be taken to ensure that the attitude of scientific enquity is applied to extra scientific domains, including questions having socio-psychological impact? Research in science education awaits answer to some of such these questions.

Thus science education, if properly conceived, should primarily be concerned with the education of the mind rather than acquisition of isolated pieces of scientific knowledge. Consequently, the vital aspects that should engage the attention of researches in science education consist in identification of these abilities and the ways and means to develop them among the young generation.

Studies Related To Attitude Towards Science

An attitude is an emotional reaction towards a person or thing. It is a personal reaction to an object, developed through experience, which can be characterised as favourable or unfavourable

An attitude is a readiness in such a way that behaviour is given a certain direction (F.S. Freeman and R.M.W. Travers)

"An attitude is relatively enduring organization of beliefs around an object or situation predisposing one to respond in some preferential manner. (Sel. 1972).

The use of science as the object or stimulus of these feelings delineates that a set of attitudes known as attitudes towards science. The scope of attitudes to be included in the definition depends on what is included in the word science.

There is a widespread belief among scientists and science educators that attitudes towards science are more negative than as desired. Declining enrolment, research reports and personal experiences have created a generally discouraging situation. The time allotted to science is not up to the expected mark and fewer students are choosing science careers. Teachers and principals in U.S.A. and many developed countries report their belief that the public's image towards science has declined in recent years. In the United States of America, national polls rank science seventh out of ten subjects in terms of usefulness in later life. Concern over the declining status of science has been voiced in the United Kingdom and Australia, as well. But the scenario is different in the developing countries. Many talented people are opting science courses as they offer valuable careers.

Studies, on attitude towards science are not readily available. Yet, certain studies having relation to the present study are given below:

Sood (1985) found the understanding of science positively related to the attitude of students towards science.

Environmental Influence Academic Achievement and Scientific Aptitude as Determinants of Adolescents' Attitude towards Science Stream (Bandopadhyay, 1984).

The main objectives of the study are the following :

1. to assess adolescent students' attitude towards science and
2. to find out the environmental and academic factors that influenced their attitude towards sceince.

The sample drawn on the basis of stratified random sampling technique consisted of 420 adolescent students, 221 boys and 199 girls from 21 school of Calcutta.

Science attitude scale of Avinash Grewal was used to study the attitude towards science.

The major findings of the study were :

1. Pupils having high positive attitude and a negative attitude towards science were different with respect to the independent variables either in isolation or in integration.
2. The obtained casual factors were environmental, attitudinal and achievement related parent education, and SES led to favourable attitude towards science. Teachers' influence, peer's influence, Vocational value of science and future aim of life were other contributory factors.

Attitude towards Physics and Cognitive preference styles among Different groups of Science students (Saxena, 1985).

The main objectives of the study were:

i) to develop a Physics Cognitive Preference Styles Test (PCPST) and Attitude towards Physics Scale (ATPS).
ii) to assess cognitive preference styles of different groups of science students.
iii) To assess the students' attitude to Physics.

iv) to study the relationship between attitudes and preference styles, and

v) to study the main and interaction effects of ('class' 'sex' and 'type of school' on attitudes and cognitive preference styles.

The 2x2x2 factorial design was used for the study.

The findings of the study were :

All the science students were found to possess a favourable attitude towards Physics.

The attitude towards Physics is positively correlated with a cognitive preference style of recalling while it is negatively correlated with applications style.

Misra, Gupta and Misra (1983) found that students are not dependent on their guardians' wishes, but they opt for science courses on their own accord, interest and future prospects.

A study of Attitude Towards learning of science among scheduled caste students (Misra, 1983).

The aim of the present study is to assess the attitude of scheduled caste students towards learning science.

Random sampling technique was used in the selection of the sample.

Science class room climate scale constructed and standardized by Sunderaranjan (1992) was used.

Findings

This study has established the significant and the positive relationship existing between the High School pupils' perceived science class room climate and their science interests. The sex of the pupils and the types of the schools were they happen to study do not themselves cause any significant difference in their sceince interests.

Minority Students in Science

This study conducted by Rankow (1986) examines the status of minority achievement and attitude towards science. It compares the attitudes of minority and white students at the age of 9, 13 and 17 using data from the 1981-82 U.S. National Assessment in Science. The author found that the minority students achieve less well in science, and have less exposure to it, but have positive attitude towards it. There is also a negative relationship between science related experience and attitude towards science.

Secondary school students attitude towards science

The main object of the study of Bance (1986) is to know the attitude of secondary school students towards science. Two types of instruments were used (questionnaire and attitude scale) 451 students' attitudes towards science were investigated to collect data.

Findings

1) In general the students hold a favourable attitude towards science.
2) The male students have more favourable attitude than female students.
3) The type of school (science school, single sex school or general secondary school) attended have an effect on the students attitudes to science. The low enrolment is not due to lack of interest or negative attitudes to the subject but may be due to some other variables that need to be investigated.

Gender differences in attitudes to science for third year pupils; an argument for single - sex teaching groups in mixed groups (Harvey and Stables, 1986).

An attitude to science scale for third year pupils in mixed and single sex schools has been developed and given to 2300 children in South West of England. This test has five components, namely attitudes to Science, Physics, Chemistry, Biology and School. The results are analysed and used to support an argument for single - sexing some school subjects in mixed schools, thus helping to include some of the better features of single sex schools in a mixed school environment.

Attitude scale comprising of 25 positive and negative items based on five point scale was prepared by researchers. There are five areas.

1. Reasons for studying science;
2. Area of interest
3. Values regarding place of science in curriculum
4. Qualities of science
5. Social relevance of science

Results obtained showed that both boys and girls (Scheduled Caste) have favourable attitude towards science.

Studies related to science education scientific aptitude and scientific attitude.

Scientific aptitude, defined as potentially for future accomplishment in science without regard to past training and achievement in the field, appears to be dependent upon a variety of factors (Bhaskar Rao, 1989). These factors are not necessarily unique to potential success in other areas. Few attempts, therefore, have been made to develop tests of aptitude for the science area alone. The Stanford Scientific Aptitude Test, first published in 1929, does however represent such an attempt. Ingenious though it was this test revealed some of the difficulties that beset an individual who undertakes the task of developing an instrument to measure scientific aptitude.

In India till 60's systematic and sustained research is lacking in the field of aptitude testing in general and measurement of scientific aptitude in particular (Sharma, 1981). Nevertheless, after the recommendations of the Secondary Education Commission were adated, interest in aptitude testing grew and some independent attempts were made by Indian researchers to standardize tests to measure scientific aptitude.

The researchers, namely Verma (1957), Mitra (1963), chowdari (1965), Nair *et al.* (1968), Deshpande (1967), Mukherji and Chatterji (1972), Gupta (1975), Ojha (1975), and Sharma (1980) developed scientific aptitude tests. (Bhaskar Rao, 1994).

Bhaskara Rao (1989) found an average scientific aptitude in secondary school students (Bhaskar Rao, 1994).

Ghose (1987) found that 70% of 9th class students possessed average scientific aptitude and about 15% each possessed high and low scientific aptitude.

Bhaskara Rao (1989) found an average level of scientific aptitude in both boys and girls.

Bhaskara Rao Digumarti (1994) found that the students of private schools, residential schools and English medium schools were better in possessing scientific aptitude than their counter parts.

The research studies on scientific aptitude indicate that there were studies in correlation with achievement and some other behavioural aspects rather studied independently. So it is better to have a look on the relationship between scientific aptitude and its correlates :

Some of the details of studies on scientific aptitude and its correlates are given below :

A critical study of Scientific Attitude and Scientific Aptitude of the Students and Determination of some Determinants of Scientific Aptitude; Ghose (1986).

The main purposes of the study were :

i) to ascertain the aptitude of the students in science with the help of specially developed scientific aptitude test.
ii) to appraise the extent of scientific attitude.
iii) to find out the extent of academic motivation of the students and SES of the parents of the students.
iv) to find out sex wise, strata wise difference in the scientific aptitude and scientific attitude of the students.
v) to find out relationships between scientific aptitude and its variables.
vi) to develop regression equation of the scientific aptitude on the independent variables identified by the researches specially constructed scientific aptitude scale and scientific attitude scale, Bhattacharya's Academic Motivation Test, Kuppuswamy's (Urban) and Pareek's (rural) SES scales were used.

ANOVA, correlation, F. test and to. test statistical techniques were used. Findings of the study were :

1) Urban students did not show better performance in the scientific aptitude than rural students.
2) Boys did not possess scientific attitude than girls.
3) There was a positive relation between scientific aptitude and scientific attitude; scientific aptitude and academic motivation; scientific attitude and academic motivation scores in scientific aptitude test could be predicted from scores in scientific attitude, academic motivation, SES of parents through multiple regression equation.
4) Students having high aptitude were superior to those having low scientific aptitude with respect to their specific aptitude.
5) Urban students belonging to the high SES group had more scientific aptitude than urban students belonging to the low SES group.
6) Rural students belonging to the high SES group did not

show better scientific aptitude than rural students belonging to low SES group.

Measurements of Aptitude for the study of Physics of the High School Science Seniors of the State of Bihar with special reference to the students of Chota Nagapur Division (Gini, 67).

The main purpose of the study was to develop a test battery to measure the aptitude for the study of Physics of the high school science seniors of the state of Bihar.

A Battery of tests having four main parts covering different areas was developed. Difficulty level, discriminative power and internal consistency of items were found out. The standardization sample was derived by adopting purposive incidentable sample technique. Reliability was calculated through split-half, K-R formula-20 and Flagan's formula. Content criterion related and factorial validity were determined. Scales and norms were prepared - Multiple correlation (R) was computed and prediction equations were prepared. Forecasting efficiency of the test was determined. The Doolittle test section method was used to select tests to form the present test battery. A test manual was prepared.

Science class room climate and interest of pupils (Sunderanjan and Rajaskhar)

Objectives : This study is intended to find out

i) the nature of relationship existing between the High School pupils perceived science class room climate and their science interests and
ii) if there is any significant difference between any two sub samples of pupils, taken at a time, in respect of their science interests.

Science Teaching in Primary Schools - a training programme, Adinarayan, (1991).

The major objectives of the study were :

i) to identify areas of competence in the teaching of elementary science.
ii) to evaluate the course in elementary science based on competency required in the teacher.
iii) to develop competency criteria for observation, investigatory and inquiry skills in pupils,
iv) to develop packages of instructional aids for teachers, and
v) to determine the advantages and effectiveness of packages in terms of development of skills in pupils.

A criterion test was developed for assessing knowledge and comprehension, observation, inquiry and investigatory skills. Reaction towards science activities was measured through a reaction scale prepared by the investigator.

The major findings were as follows :

1. There was a significant difference in the development of skills among students in the experimental group.
2. Class IV students in nine schools and class V students in seven schools of experimental group indicated an increase in knowledge and comprehension in comparison to control group of students.
3. The experimental group greatly favoured science activities.

Chatterjee, *et al* (1972) found a very high degree of correlation between biographical factors and achievement and aptitude for the technical stream.

Crawfold (1960) with standard Scientific Aptitude Test reported a correlation of 0.3 between scores earned on this test by entering students and their first grades or marks in science and pre-engineering courses.

In support of this finding, Bernett, Seashore and Weisman (1960), the constructors of the Differential Aptitude Tests, found that the success in science shows highest correlation with verbal reasoning, numerical ability and certain aspects of language aptitude.

The Guilford - Zimmerman Aptitude Survey (1950) also revealed that there was significant relationship between science achievement and science aptitude.

General ability, scientific aptitude/reasoning and problem solving ability were significantly responsible for the learning of science (Pal 1982)

Pillai, Thakur and Joseph found that there was a significant positive relationship among science achievement scientific aptitude and intelligence.

Sree kumar (1972), Chatterjee, *et al* (1978) and Sujatha (1987) identified a positive relationship among scientific aptitude, science interest and science achievement.

Studies of Ganguly, *et al*, (1972) Nain and Joseph (1988) and Skaria (1984) revealed that scientific aptitude was highly associated with academic success.

The studies of Zyne (1929) Bertòn and Perry (1975) on

predictive value of Stanford Scientific Aptitude Test found that scientific aptitude can be employed for predicting science achievement.

Gupta states that science achievement has a significant role to play in predicting scientific aptitude.

A review of the past studies which was related mostly to the present problem provided an insight into selection of proper method, for selection of tool and for selection of sample, collection of data and its analysis. The review also helped the investigator in describing the method which would be useful for the present study.

The studies reviewed reveal that many researches have been undertaken on attitude towards different subjects, but regarding science subject not many were found with the sample of prospective science teachers in context of scientific aptitude SES, and personality traits.

It would be worthwhile to measure the attitude towards science subject and explore its relationship with other potential variabl‹ s and thereby suggest some programmes to be undertaken by the future researchers in the field of attitude towards science.

Planning and Procedure

Introduction

A survey was undertaken in order to explore the attitude of prospective secondary school science teachers towards science subject. In order to achieve fruitful results, detailed planning is required for any research work. Planning of the work depends on procedure. Selection of appropriate research method helps in proper analysis, interpretation and drawing of conclusions. This chapter which deals with planning presents the methods of research, the sample for the study, the nature of the variables hypotheses and the statistical techniques to be adopted.

Methods of Research

How to select appropriate method and technique of research for a particular problem is the most important aspect of the research. The method selected must be helpful in studying a particular problem. Sukhia, (1965) have classified methods of educational research as under :

A. The Historical method
B. The normative survey method
C. The experimental method, and
D. The comparative or collection or genetic method.

A. The Historical Method : The historical method deals with the events, persons and places of the past.

B. The Normative Survey Method : George J. Mouly has said "No category of educational research is more widely used than the type. Known variously as the survey, the normative survey, status and description research. The broad classification comprises of a variety of specific techniques and procedures, all similar from the stand point of purpose - that is, to establish the stauts of the phenomenon under investigation".

Normative survey method of investigation attempts to discribe and interpret what exists at present in the form of conditions, practices, processes, trends, effects, attitudes, beliefs. etc. It investigates into the conditions or relationships that exist; practices that prevail; beliefs, point of views or attitudes that are held, processes that are going on; influences that are felt and trends that are developing. It is an organized attempt to analyse, to interpret and report the present status of a social institution, group or area. The normative studies differ from other studies. Historical studies deal with the past, where was survey deals with the present. Surveys differ from experimental studies in purpose. Surveys are oriented towards the determination of the status of a given phenomenon rather than towards the isolation of causative factors. Survey studies differ from case studies in that surveys are generally broad and large, cross-selectional samples, while case studies are oriented to more intensive and longitudinally studies of a smaller sample.

Worthwhile survey studies collect the following types of information :

(i) of what exists by studying and analyzing important aspect of the present situation.

(ii) of what we want by clarifying goals and objectives possibly otherwise considerable to be desirable, and

(iii) of how to get here through discovering the possible means of achieving goals on the basis of the experiences of others or the opinions of experts.

The characteristics of survey are :

1. It is cross-sectional.
2. It gathers information from a relatively large number of cases.
3. It is concerned not with the characteristics of individuals but with generalised statistics of the whole population or a representative sample.
4. It deals with clearly defined problems and has definite objectives. It requires an imaginative planning, a careful

analysis and interpretation of the data and a logical and skilful reporting of the findings.

5. It is more realistic than the experiment in that it investigates phenomena in their natural setting.
6. Surveys may be qualitative or quantitative.
7. Description resulting from surveys may be either verbal or expressed in mathematical symbols.

C. *Experimental Method* : This method is classical method of science laboratory which needs an analysis of what will be and what will occur under controlled conditions.

D. *The Causal Comparative Methods* : The comparative method seeks for causes and effects of the phenomenon. The correlation method analyses relationship between data, variables and results, while the case study aims at gathering of information about a single person, institution, family cultural group or community. The genetic method investigates the biological and psychological phenomenon of changes, growth and development.

Selection of Research Method for the Study

The present study is the attitude of prospective secondary school science teachers towards science subject. This involves a large sample. And the study is the cross-section of the situation. Therefore, survey method is the most appropriate method and the study was conducted using survey method of research.

Selection of Research Tools

A research tool plays a major role in any worthwhile research as it is the sole factor in determining the sound data and in arriving at perfect conclusion about the problem or study in hand, which ultimately helps in providing suitable remedial measures to the problem concerned. Selection of the tool is a major task and one should take care in the selection of tools.

As the study is the survey of the attitude of prospective secondary school science teachers towards science subject, a thorough and in depth study of the various works related to attitude was made. Greater interest was shown in the attitudional studies regarding science subject at different levels.

After studying different studies the researcher has selected science attitude scale developed by Avinash Grewal as the most appropriate tool to know the attitude of prospective secondary school science teachers towards science subject.

Selection of Variables

Along with attitude other related variables were also selected, namely :

1. Sex
2. Methods of teaching
3. Area
4. Scientific aptitude
5. S E S
6. Personality traits
   a) Self-sufficiency Vs dependency
   b) Dominance Vs submissiveness
   c) Introversion Vs extroversion
   d) Emotional stability

All these were taken as independent variables and attitude towards science subject was taken as dependent variable. The rationale for choosing the above stated variables was discussed herewith.

Sex

In olden days the male were educated and the female were restricted to their kitchens Times changed and the importance of women education is recognized. In the words of our late Prime Minister Jawaharlal Nehru, "If you educate a man you educate only one person; if you educate a woman you educate the entire family". In course of time women education gained importance and most of the parents encouraging their daughters to pursue higher education. The women are also showing excellence in all fields.

As the psychological conditions, exposure to the society, education and other aspects of male and female are very different there may be a significant difference in their attitude towards science subject, scientific aptitudes, and different personality traits.

Methods of Teaching

Science education in Colleges of Education is divided into two branches, viz. 1. Physical sciences - which concern with material things, and 2. Biological or life sciences - which concern with living organisms. Prospective science teachers select either physical science education or biological science education in their training period depending on the subjects studied by them at graduation level. Selection of science subjects at +2 level and graduation level involves the attitude and aptitude towards these subjects. Hence there may be difference in the attitude of prospective physical science and biological science teachers.

Area

The urban colleges are well equipped in many aspects. The buildings, the libraries, the laboratories, the teaching staff, the educational atmosphere, the competitive spirit among students, the amenities provided to students to pursue education, the exposure to science fairs, exhibitions work shops, etc. the use of audio aids, are always better in urban colleges than in rural colleges. The library, laboratory facilities play a commendable role in the acquisition of attitude towards science subject and scientific aptitude. A comparison between urban and rural students brings out the difference in the level of possession of attitude towards science subject, if there is any.

Description of Tools

Science Attitude Scale

A review of the attitude scales revealed that many attitude scales have been prepared in the last three decades to study the attitudes of people towards different issues like co-education, tuition classes, physical education, micro teaching, different disciplines at secondary school level like new mathematics, science, etc. Regarding attitude towards science, tests were developed by J.K. Sood, Allen Hugh Jr., Avinash Grewal, etc.

Out of the available tests on attitude towards science in terms of (1) positively intellectual (2) negatively intellectual (3) positively emotional (4) negatively emotional attitudes. The scale was constructed using Likert method of summated rating scale.

There are twenty items in SAS. Out of 20 items 10 items are positively stated (S.No. 2,4,6,8,10,12,14,16,18,20) and 10 items are negatively stated (S.No. 1,3,5,7,9,11,13,15,17,19). Positive items are assigned weight rangling from 4 (strongly agree) to zero(strongly disagree). In the case of ten negative items scoring is reversed ranging from zero (strongly agree) to four (strongly disagree). The attitude score of a subject is the sum total of scores of all the twenty items of the scale.

The reliability of Science Attitude Scale (SAS) was estimated by the split half (0.86) and test retest (0.75) which was found to be quite satisfactory.

The SAS appears to have content validity and the method of selecting items supports this. In addition, difference in mean scores were found among the selected groups of known preference for science, i.e. Arts (Means = 46.41) and Science (Means = 50.51) students which is high (t = 6.6) at 1 percent level.

Scientific Aptitude Scale

A review of the scientific aptitude tests revealed that there were tests developed by Verma, Mitra, Choudari, Deshpande, Mukherji and Chatterji, Gupta, Ohja Sharma, Agarwal, Nairetal, and A.K.P. Sinha and L. N. K. Sinha.

Out of these tests available on scientific aptitude the Scientific Aptitude Test for college students of A.K.P. Sinha and L.N.K. Sinha was selected for the use in the present study originally it was prepared in Hindi, later the researcher translated into English language. The details of the test were given below :

The test consists of seven area, viz., (1) Experimental belt, (2) Detection of in consistencies or illogical conclusion (3) Ability to deduce conclusions from the data provided (4) Accuracy of interpretation (5) Ability to reason and solve the problems (6) Caution and thoroughness (7). Accuracy of observation. The components of the test, number of items, weightage for each area are given below:

The validity of the test was determined by computing correlation between the composite scores on the test and the university examination work.

The test retest reliability for a sample of 58 is found 0.81. Total scores of the test were used for assessing temporal stability. The reatest period was 3 weeks approximately.

Norms for three groups. i) Selected scientific group (N-96) (2). Unselected scientific group (N=396) and non scientific group N=100 are presented in the given table.

Weightages Given to Different Area

Area	*No. of items*	*Weightage*	*Max. Weightage score*
1. Experimental belt	5	3	15
2. Detention of inconsistencies of illogical conclusions	7	3	21
3. Ability to deduce conclusion from the data provided	6	7	42
4. Accuracy of interpretation	4	2	8
5. Ability to reason and solve problem	7	7	49
6. Caution and thoroughness	4	5	20
7. Accuracy of observation	1	3	3
Total No. of items	34		

Norms for the different group

Group	*N*	*M*	*SD*	*SE*
1. Selected Scientific Group	96	153.55	10.54 - +1.08	
2. Unselected Scientific Group	396	119.45	27.60 - +1.39	
3. Non Scientific Group	100	61.60	41.70	+4.17

This test would undoubtedly serve as a reliable and valid instrument to measure the scientific aptitude of prospective science teachers.

Socio Economic Status Scale

Socio Economic Status is defined as social prestige enjoyed by means of education, occupation and economic status. Socio Economic Status of Beena Shah was used to measure the SES of prospective science teachers. The scale consists of items covering different aspects like Caste, Occupation, Education, Income, Possession, and Social participation. The details about the variables and their scoring procedure are given below:

The weightage to different caste groups is given, as-scheduled caste (1), Scheduled tribe (2), Backward caste (3), Christian and other Non-Hindu Groups (4), Vaishyas and Kshatriyas (5), and Brahmins (6).

Occupation has been categorized into five major categories

on the continuum of occupational prestige. 1. Score, Category 4 (skilled work, etc.) - 2 scores, category 3 (clerk, etc.) - 4 scores, category 4 (Non Gazetted Officer, etc.) - 8 Scores, Category 5 (Gazetted Officer, etc.) - 12 score. The occupation of the father/ guardian, mother and main occupation of the family are taken as the indicators of occupational status.

The eight categories of qualifications with their score illiterate (0) Primary pass (1) High school pass (2), Intermediate/High School + some post High school diploma (3), B.A./B.Sc./B.Ed./ P.G. etc. (5) M.Ed./M.B.B.S./B.E. etc. (6), Ph.D./M.S./M.D./M.E., etc. (7) They are arranged from illiterated to professional Post - Graduate degrees. The weightage assigned varies from 0 to 7. The educational status score is the average of the scores of the father, mother and sibling. Income is an index of economic status.

Ownership of house, number of rooms, house-hold materials like news papers and magazines animals and acres of land.

These are the six indicators of possession, six questions are given on the basis of the quantity of the possessions.

Being a member of some association, award of honours, titles etc. and involvement of these things effects the social status of person.

The composite SES score is defined as the sum of the scores obtained on the above six variables i.e. Caste, Occupation, Education, Income, Possession and Social participation.

The value of reliability coefficients were derived with the help of test - retest method and were found to be highly significant which are presented in below given table:

Test - Retest method

Time Interval	*N*	*Reliability coefficiency*	*Reliability Index*
20 days	225	0.92	0.96
30 days	225	0.89	0.94

To assess the validity of this SES scale correlation coefficients of scores obtained on these six components variable with composite SES scores were calculated. The values are given in below Table, Correlation coefficients between total SES scores and scores on its component variables.

Corr. Coef	*Caste*	*Occupation*	*Education*	*Income*	*Possession*	*Social Status*
n	0.72	0.82	0.86	0.83	0.78	0.69

The values of correlation coefficients between composite SES scores on individual six component variables were high and statistically significant far beyond 0.0001 level of significance. This indicates that the validity of this SES measures is high order.

Since the reliability and validity of this SES scale is of high order, it can be side with confidence that this measure will assess of one's socio-economic status whether belonging to high & low SES.

Self Sufficiency Vs. Dependency

A person who expresses his own thoughts and ideas by himself without taking the help of others is said to be a self sufficient person. A person who amities others and relies upon others for his thoughts and expressions is called a dependent person. A self sufficient person will not only express whatever comes into his mind but will tackle any problem, emotional or mental, that he encounters in life.

It is assumed that persons indicating self sufficient personality trait may have positive attitude towards science subjects. Some of the behavioural characteristics appear to be very close to each other. The behavioural characteristics of a self sufficient person are as follows : -

- can discharge the duty entrusted to him.
- tries to solve the problems in his life.
- has high confidence in him to face any situation in life.
- never in search of undue help from others.

A person is said to be dependent when he possesses the following behavioural characteristics :

- generally depends on others for his work. hardly helps others is conventional.
- always seeks guidance from others.
- invites instructions from others to get away with his problems.
- shifts his responsibilities to others.
- keeps problems pending for quite a longer time.

The researcher tried to find out the effect of self sufficiency Vs dependency personality trait on the attitude of prospective science teachers towards science subject.

Self Sufficiency Vs. Dependency Scale

For measuring the self sufficiency Vs dependency trait of the prospective science teachers. The investigator has selected the self-sufficiency Vs dependency scale constructed and standardized by A.S.Patel.

The scale has 10 statements which are to be responded in two categories "Yes" or "No". A positively worded statement checked into "Yes" category gets one mark and a negatively worded statement checked into 'No' category also gets one mark. Hence the score varies between 0 and 10.

Dominance Vs. Submissions

Dominants are aggressive, competitive, rigid, less acceptable tendency and initiative. Submissive people are generally mild accommodative shy and easily acceptable ones.

Dominance Vs. Submissiveness Scale.

For measuring dominance Vs submissiveness of prospective science teachers the investigator has selected the Dominance Vs submissiveness scale constructed and standardized by A.S.Patel.

This scale has 10 statements which are to be responded in two categories, "Yes" or "No" . A positively worded statement checked into "Yes" category gets one mark and a negatively worded statement checked into 'No' category also gets one mark. Hence the score varies between 0 and 10 .

Extroversion Vs. Introversion

Extroverts are out going, relatively uninhibited, and their activities bring them into contact with other people, and there are not attracted by solitary pursuits. Introverts tend to possess the opposites of these qualities. Qualities which characterise the introvert, such as persistence, rigidity, subjectivity, shyness and irritability are known as introvert traits.

Introversion Vs. Extroversion Scale

For measuring the Introversion Vs. extroversion of the prospective secondary school science teachers the researcher has selected the Introversion Vs. extroversion Scale constructed and standardized by A.S.Patel.

The scale has 20 statements which are to be responded in two categories, 'Yes' or 'No' . A positively worded statement checked into "Yes" category gets one mark and a negatively worded statement checked into 'No' category also gets one mark. Hence the score varies between 0 and 20.

Emotional Stability

Emotional stability refers to the type of behaviours which is free from neurotic symptoms. A person having this trait has a realistic view about life. He is a mentally matured person. He tries to face the ups and downs of the life. He tries to reason out things and solves problems with patience. Emotionally unstable person's general behaviour is full of neurotic symptoms like evasiveness and immaturity. Emotionally unstable persons react in a appropriately without viewing a situation. They are more sensitive and tonely about the issue of life. The emotionally unstable persons are easily teased and are often frustrated. They often find engrained themselves in life problems. This description of emotionally stable and unstable persons helps us to assure that the behavioural characteristics of emotionally stable persons correspond to the characteristics of positive attitude towards science subject. Therefore, the investigator selected emotional stability trait of personality to explore its possible effect on the attitude of prospective science teachers towards science subject.

Emotional Stability Scale

For measuring emotional stability of the prospective science teachers, the investigator has selected the emotional stability scale constructed and standardized by A.S.Patel.

The scale has 10 statements which are to be responded in two categories, 'Yes' and 'No' . A positively worded statement checked into "Yes" category gets one mark and a negatively worded statement checked into 'No' category also gets one mark. Hence the score varies between O and 10.

Selection of Sample

The next step in conducting the study in selection of sample and administration of the selected tools on them. The population for this study refers to all science students who seek admission into Colleges of Education after passing the Education Common Entrance Test (EdCET). As it is not economical. feasible and possible to collect data from the whole population, the researcher has decided to select a representative sample. With the help of this sample, the findings can be generalised for the whole population. While selecting the sample the researcher kept the following points in mind.

1. Sample should represent both the sexes.
2. Sample should represent the area, i.e. urban and rural.
3. The sample size should be fairly large to give a proper representation and to depict a real picture.

Keeping the above points in view and with the experience and advice of the experts, the researcher has decided to take a large sample nearly five hundred. To make the results reliable, suitable method of sampling has been employed. After studying the pros and cons of different methods of sampling, like random sampling, purposive sampling, multi-stage sampling, like random sampling method and purposie cluster sampling method, the researcher has decided that cluster sampling technique is the most suitable one. A brief up of the cluster sampling technique is as follows.

Cluster Sampling

This method is useful when the selections of an individual member of the population is practicable. In this method instead of an individual a group or a cluster of members are selected as the sample. It is explained by William Wiersma (1976) as:

"Cluster sampling is a procedure of selection in which the unit of selection called the cluster contains two or more population members. Each member of the population may be uniquely identified with one and only one cluster. Cluster sampling is useful in situations where there is a natural group of the population and this considered as a cluster. The samples are randomly selected from the larger population of cluster.

Once the cluster is selected, then all the members in the cluster are included in the sample. There is no need of having even number of individuals in all the clusters. Each college of Education has been considered as a cluster.

The sample was collected from 5 Colleges of Education located in Krishna and Guntur District of Andhra Pradesh. These prospective teachers took admission into B.Ed. course only after passing the Ed. CET. These prospective teachers consist of both male and female trainees coming from rural and urban areas with varying aptitude, SES and personality traits.

Administration of the Tools

The selected tools were personally administered on 500 prospective science teachers who opted either physical science or biological sciences as one of the methods of teaching.

Hypotheses

Selection of research method and sample help to pave a proper way to conduct the research. But, the most critical and important aspect of the research is formation of Hypotheses.

It gives direction to the research work. Research without hypotheses is like roaming in a forest without knowing the way to come out.

Hypothesis is nothing but a tentative supposition or assumption. It is a temporary guess or statement made by the research which has to be tested.

Hypothesis may be defined as a proposition or a set of propositions set forth an explanation for the occurrence of some specified group of phenomena either asserted merely as a provisional conecture to guide some investigation or accepted as highly probable in the light of established facts. Quite often a research hypothesis is a predictive statement capable of being tested by scientific methods. Hypothesis may be broadly classified into two major categories, Null hypothesis and Alternative hypothesis.

Null Hypothesis and alternative hypothesis

If we proceed on the assumption that both groups are equally good then this assumption is termed as the null hypothesis. As against this we may think that both groups are not equal and there is difference in both the groups we are then setting what is termed as alternative hypothesis. The null hypothesis is generally symbolized as Ho and the alternative hypothesis as Ha.

Rejecting the null hypothesis is known as alternative hypothesis. In other words the set of alternative to the null hypothesis is referred to as the alternative hypothesis.

In the choice of NULL hypothesis, the following considerations are usually kept in view :

a) Alternative hypothesis is usually the one which wishes to prove and the null hypothesis is the one which wishes to disprove, thus a null hypothesis represents the hypothesis we are trying to reject, and alternative hypothesis represents all other possibilities.

b) if the rejection of a certain hypothesis when it is actually true involves great risk, it is taken as null hypothesis because then the probability of rejecting it when it is true is L (the level of significance) which is chosen very small.

c) Null hypothesis should always be specific hypothesis i.e. it should not state about or approximately a certain value. On account of the above reasons researcher has employed null hypothesis for the present study.

5

Data Collection and Presentation

Introduction

The task of data collection begins after a research problem has been defined and research design chalked out. While deciding about the method of data collection to be used for the study, the researcher should keep in mind the sources of data. The sources of information are generally classified as primary and secondary. Primary sources include the actual information received from the individuals directly concerned with the problem of the study.

As planned, the researcher has adopted the survey method of research and used predesigned and tested tools for collecting the sample. The selected tools were administered on 500 prospective science teaches. These tools were administered personally on science trainees who opted either physical science or biological science as one of the methods of teachings in their B.Ed. course. After administration and evaluation of the tools the researcher was leftout with only 458 usable sample.

Distribution of Primary data

The sample of 458 was collected from five B.Ed. college of Andhra Pradesh. These prospective science teachers took admission into B.Ed. course only after passing the EDCET (Education Common Entrance Test).

They compute both male and female trainees coming from urban and rural areas. The distribution of prospective science teachers in different instructions is presented in table 5.1 given below:

Table 5.1
Distribution of Prospective Science Teachers in Different Institutions

Sr. No.	Name of the Institutions	No. of prospective science teachers		
		Male	Female	Total
1.	Andhra Luthern College of Education, Guntur	55	33	85
2.	Montessori Mahila college of Education, Vijayawada	—	110	110
3.	Rayapati Venkata Ranga Rao Rao College of Education, Guntur	52	37	89
4.	Siddhartha College of Education, Vijayawada	52	32	84
5.	St. Josephs College of Education for women, Guntur	—	90	90
		159	299	458

Variable-wise Distribution or Primary Data

The collected sample is classified separately on the basis of sex, methods of teaching and area. These tables are presented in Tables 5.2.1, 5.2.2, 5.2.3.

Table 5.2.1
Sex-wise Distribution of Prospective Science Teachers

Male	Famale	Total
159	299	458

Table 5.2.2
Methodology-wise Distribnution of Prospective Science Teachers

Physical science	Biological science	Total
222	236	458

Table 5.2.3
Area-wise distribution of Prospective Science Teachers

Urban	Rural	Total
263	195	458

Independent Variables

The distribution tables of the other independent variables, namely sex methods of teaching, area, scientific attitude, SES self sufficiency dependency, dominance vs. submission introversion vs. extroversion and emotional stability are presented along with their mean, median and S.D. in tables 5.4; 5.5; 5.6; 5.7; 5.8; 5.9, 5.10; 5.11 and 5.12. The rationale for selection of these independent variables tools used for the study are discussed in detail in chapter IV planning and procedure.

Presentation of Collected Data

The Primary data that was collected from different institution was 458. But to use 2x2x2 factorial design the usable data remained to be 192. This data has been tabulated to test the various hypotheses of the present study.

Dependent Variable

The frequency distribution table of the dependent variable, viz., attitude towards science subject, is given below along with its mean, median and S.D. in table 5.3:

Table 5.3
Frequency Distribution of Attitude Scores with Mean, Median and S.D.

Sr. No.	*Class Interval*	*Frequency*
1.	75-79	1
2.	70-74	4
3.	65-69	5
4.	60-64	4
5.	55-59	15
6.	50-54	32
7.	45-49	62
8.	40-44	42
9.	35-39	22
10.	30-34	5

N= 192
Mean = 48.54
Median = 47.26
S.D. = 8.29

Table 5.4
Sex-wise Frequency Distribution of Attitude Scores

Sr. No.	*Class Interval*	*Frequency* *Female*	*Male*
1.	75-79	1	1
2.	70-74	1	2
3.	65-69	1	3
4.	60-64	2	3
5.	55-59	9	6
6.	50-54	22	10
7.	45-49	34	28
8.	40-44	19	23
9.	35-39	6	16
10.	30-34	1	4

		Male	Female
N	=	96	96
Mean	=	47.82	49.2
Median	=	46.5	47.7
S.D.	=	7.02	9.32

Table 5.5
Methods of Teaching-wise Frequency Distribution of Attitude Scores

S.N.	*Class Interval*	*Frequency* *Physical*	*Biological*
1.	75-79	1	1
2.	70-84	2	1
3.	65-69	2	1
4.	60-64	3	3
5.	55-59	9	6
6.	50-54	16	16
7.	45-49	29	33
8.	40-44	22	20
9.	35-39	8	14
10.	30-34	4	1

		Biological science	Physical science
N	=	96	96
Mean	=	47.9	49.2
Median	=	46.5	46.9
S.D.	=	7.6	8.87

Table 5.6
Area-wise Frequency Distribution of Attitude Scores

S.NO.	*Class Interval*	*Frequency*	
		Urban	*Rural*
1.	75-79	1	1
2.	70-74	1	1
3.	65-69	2	2
4.	60-64	3	3
5.	55-59	7	8
6.	50-54	17	15
7.	45-49	28	34
8.	40-44	24	18
9.	35-39	12	10
10.	30-34	1	4

		Urban	Rural
N	=	96	96
Mean	=	48.50	48.5
Median	=	46.51	46.5
S.D.	=	8.59	7.9

Table 5.7
Frequency Distribution Mean, Median, S.D. and N onscores of Scientific Aptitude

S.No.	*Class Interval*	*Frequency*
1	90-99	12
2	80-89	13
3	70-79	16
4	60-69	19
5	50-59	29
6	40-49	44
7	30-39	37
8	20-29	18
9	10-19	4

N	=	192
Mean	=	51.04
Median	=	44.56
S.D.	=	21.12

Table 5.8
Frequency Distribution, Mean, Median S.D. and N on Scores of SES

S.No.	*Class Interval*	*Frequency*
1	90-99	5
2	80-89	5
3	70-79	7
4	60-69	11
5	50-59	20
6	40-49	65
7	30-39	46
8	20-29	24
9	10-19	10
	total	192

N = 192
Mean = 48.5
Median = 41.26
S.D. = 17.78

Table 5.9
Frequency Distribution, Mean, Median S.D. and N on Scores of Self-sufficiency vs. Dependency Personality Trait.

S.No.	*Class Interval*	*Frequency*
1	9 - 10	10
2	7 - 8	54
3	5 - 6	77
4	3 - 4	45
5	1 - 2	6
		192

N = 192
Mean = 5.3
Median = 6.3
S.D. = 2.6

Table 5.10

Frequency Distribution, Mean, Median S.D. and N on Scores of Self-sufficiency vs. Dependency Personality Trait.

S.No.	*Class Interval*	*Frequency*
1	9 - 10	4
2	7 - 8	48
3	5 - 6	88
4	3 - 4	46
5	1 - 2	6
		192

N = 192
Mean = 5.49
Median = 5.9
S.D. = 2.68

Table 5.11

Frequency Distribution, Mean, Median S.D. and N on Scores of Introversion vs. Extroversion Personality Trait.

S.No.	*Class Interval*	*Frequency*
1	18 -19	2
2	16 -17	4
3	14 -15	12
4	12 -13	46
5	10 -11	50
6	8 - 9	39
7	6 -7	27
8	4 - 5	10
9	2 - 3	2
		192

N = 192
Mean = 9.76
Median = 9.9
S.D. = 2.67

Table 5.12
Frequency Distribution Mean, Median S.D. and N on Scores of Emotional Personality Trait

S.No.	*Class Interval*	*Frequency*
1	10-11	84
2	8- 9	62
3	6- 7	46
4	4 -5	42
5	2- 3	8
		192

N = 192
Mean = 6.2
Median = 5.7
S.D. = 2.25

Analysis of the dependent variable attitude scores, testing the null hypotheses and interpretation are carried in chapter VI.

Analysis and Interpretation

Introduction

In this study the collected data was used to study the effect of independent variables, viz., sex, methods of teaching, area, scientific aptitude, SES and selected personality traits. The scores of the attitude towards science subject were considered as the dependent variable.

As three independent variables were taken at a time for the study factorial design of 2x2x2 is used. Sex and methods of teaching were taken as common independent variables. Hence, they are seen common in all the studies. Figural representation of the groups formed on the basis of two levels of sex, methods of teaching and psycho-social variables is presented below in Table 6.1.

Table 6.1

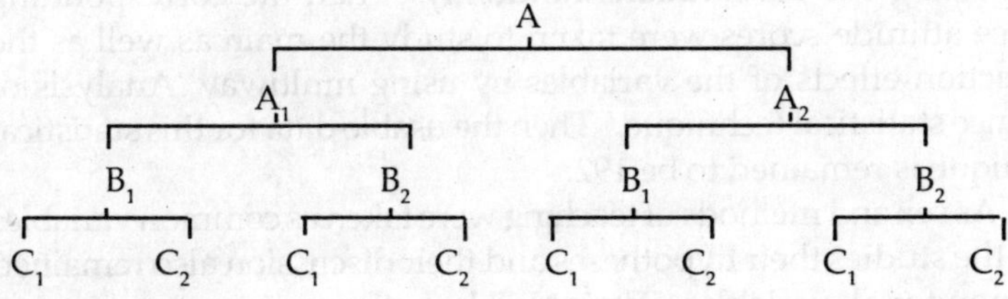

A = Sex

A_1 = Male

A_2 = Female

B = Methods of teaching
B_1 = Physical Science
B_2 = Biological Science

C = 1 Area
C_1 = Urban
C_2 = Rural

2 Scientific Aptitude
3 SES
4 Self sufficiency Vs. dependency
5 Dominance Vs. submissiveness
6 Introversion Vs. extroversion
7 Emotional stability

The data was collected from 500 prospective science teachers of Andhra Pradesh. But the usable data remained to be 458. Parametric techniques were studied in detail and finally came to a decision that Analysis of Variance/'F'-test was more appropriate after giving due consideration to the 458 observations and the independent variables.

As stated earlier, each independent variable was analysed separately and presented as its corresponding study. In each study sex and methods of teaching were taken as the two common independent variables and the third independent variable kept changing. There by 2x2x2 factorial design is selected, and the scores of attitude towards science subject was treated as dependent variable.

The 458 observations when divided at two levels of the three independent variables, eight cells were formed. It was found that the number of observations in each cell were not equal, hence the minimum number was selected. Later, all the cells were made equal by selecting the observations randomly. Then the corresponding science attitude scores were taken to study the main as well as the interaction effects of the variables by using multiway 'Analysis of variance statistical technique.' Then the usable data for this statistical technique is remained to be 192.

As sex and methods of teaching were taken as common variables in all the studies their hypotheses and their discussion also remained common for all variables. Their Null hypotheses were states as :

H_{01} : There is no significant main effect of sex on attitude towards science subject.

H_{02} : There is no significant main effect of methods of teaching on attitude towards science subject.

H_{04} : There is no significant interaction effect between sex and methods of teaching on attitude towards science subject.

The tools and the sample used for the study were already discussed in chapter IV. The strategy adopted, and final number of observations used for analysis were also stated in the beginning of this chapter.

Study

Area and Attitude towards science subject

The hypotheses formulated for testing are given below: Hypotheses 1,2 and 4 remain the same as given in para 6.1.0.

H_{03} : There is no significant main effect of area on attitude towards science subject.

H_{05} : There is no significant interaction effect between sex and area on attitude towards science subject.

H_{06} : There is no significant interaction effect between methods of teaching and area on attitude towards science subject.

H_{07} : There is no significant interaction effect among sex, methods of teaching and are an attitude science subject.

Table 6.2

ΣX and $\bar{X}$ of the Scores of the Independent Variables of the Eight Groups Formed on the Basis of Two Levels of Sex, Methods of Teaching and Area on the Scores of Attitude Towards Science Subject.

	Sex (A)			
	Male (A_1)		*Female (A_2)*	
Area (c)	*Physical Science (B_2)*	*Biological Science (B_2)*	*Physical Science (B_1)*	*Biological Science (B_2)*
Urban (C_1)	A_1 B_1 C_1	A_1 B_2 C_1	A_2 B_1 C_1	A_2 B_2 C_1
N	24	24	24	24
ΣX	1180	1101	1172	1198
$\bar{X}$	49.20	45.90	49.85	49.84
Rural (C_2)	A_1 B_1 C_2	A_1 B_2 C_2	A_2 B_1 C_2	A_2 B_2 C_2
N	24	24	24	24
ΣX	1175	1098	1189	1195
$\bar{X}$	48.96	45.79	49.55	49.79

Sample and Strategy

The sample of 458 observations when divided into eight cells as per the factorial design the minimum found was only 24. On equalizing all the cells with minimum number of the remained to be only 192 observations. Strategy and analysis remained the same as discussed previously. The primary data like the number of observations in each cell, their sum and their means are presented in table 6.2. The summary of ANOVA was prepared primary statistical data is furnished in table 6.3.

Table 6.3
Summary of Analysis of Variance of Independent Variables Sex, Methods of Teaching and Area on Attitude Towards Science Subject

Source	*Sum-SQR*	*D.F.*	*Mean-Sum-SQR*	*F-Value*	*Remark*
A	99.15625	1	99.15625	1.46197	N.S.
B	85.32291	1	85.32291	1.25801	N.S.
C	0.32292	1	0.32292	0.00476	N.S.
A*B	379.71875	1	379.71875	5.59860	X
A*C	157.71875	1	157.71875	2.32542	N.S
B*C	8.34375	1	8.34375	0.12302	N.S.
A*B*C	7.48958	1	7.48958	0.11043	N.S.
ERROR	%12479.58301	184	67.82382	1.00000	

A = Sex
B = Methods of teaching
C Area
With df. 1 and 184 F Value at 0.05 level = 3.91
with df. 1 and 184 F Value at 0.01 level = 6.81
X Significant at 0.05 level
XX Significant at 0.01 level
N.S. Not significant

Discussion

H_{01} There is no significant main effect of sex on attitude of prospective science teacher towards science subject.

The obtained 'F' value of sex as a main effect is 1.46 as seen in table 6.3. The table value of 'F' at 0.05 level is 3.91 and at 0.01 level is 6.81 with df 1 and 184. The obtained value is much below the table value of 'F'. Hence H_{01} is accepted and inferred that there is no significant main effect of sex on the attitude of prospective science teachers. It is clear that whether they are male or female science teachers they do not show much difference in the attitude towards science subject and it is inferred that sex does not play any role in developing attitude towards science subject.

Table 6.4
Means of Male and Female Teachers

Sex (A)	*Means*	*Mean Difference*
Male (A_1)	47.80	1.40
Female (A_2)	49.20	

The means of scores of male and female are derived from the data and presented in Table 6.4. To test the hypothesis, further the means in the Table are examined. The apparent mean difference of 1.4. The difference that is seen may be due to sampling error or measurement or other factors. Hence, it is inferred that there is no significant difference in the attitude of male and female science teachers towards science subject.

H_{02} : There is no significant main effect of methods of teaching on attitude of prospective science teachers towards science subject.

The obtained 'F' value of methods of teaching as a main effect is 1.2 as seen in table 6.3. The table value of 'F' at 0.05 level is 3.91 and 0.01 level is 6.81 with df/1 and 184. The obtained 'F' value is below the table value of 'F' at 0.05 level is 3.91 and at 0.01 level is 6.81 with df 1 and 184. The obtained value is much below the table value of 'F'. Hence H_{02} is accepted and inferred that there is no significant main effect of sex on the attitude of prospective science teachers towards science.

To confirm the hypothesis further the means of physical science and biological science teachers attitude scores are examined as given in table 6.5.

The apparent means difference between physical science and biological science teachers is 1.33. This is may be due to other factors. Hence, it is inferred that there is no significant difference in the attitudes of physical science teachers and biological science teacher towards science subject.

H_{03} : There is no significant main effect of area on attitude of prospective science teachers towards science subject.

The obtained 'F' value of the area as a main effect is 0.004 as seen in table 6.3. This value is much below the table value of 'F' at 0.05 level which is 3.91. Hence H_{03} is accepted. It is clear that area has no main effect on attitude o propsoective science teachers. Whether the teachers came from urban or rural area they hardly show any difference in developing attitude towards science subject.

Table 6.5
Means of Physical Science and Biological Science Teachers

Method of teaching (B)	*Means*	*M.D.*
Physical Science (B_1)	49.20	1.33
Biological Science (B_2)	47.87	

Table 6.6
Means of Urban and Rural Science Teachers

Area (c)	*Mean*	*M.D.*
Urban (C_1)	48.58	0.08
Rural (C_2)	48.50	

To test this hypothesis further the means of urban and rural teachers attitude scores given in table 6.6 are examined. The apparent mean difference 0.08 is not significant. Hence it is concluded that there is no significant difference in the attitudes of urban science teachers and rural science teacher towards science subject.

Interaction Effects

H_{04} : There is no significant interaction effect between sex and methods of teaching on the attitude of prospective science teachers towards science subject.

It is seen from table 6.3 that the obtained 'F' value of the interaction effect of sex and methods of teaching is 5.59. The value of 'F' at 0.05 level is 3.91 and at 0.01 level is 6.81 with df 1 and 184. Hence H_{04} is rejected and inferred that sex and methods of teaching interact with each other on attitude towards science subject.

Table 6.7

Dischotomised Means of Sex and Methods of Teaching

Method of teaching (B)	*Physical Science*	*Biological Science*
Sex (A)	(B_1)	(B_2)
Male (A_1)	A_1B_1 49.89	A_1B_2 45.34
Female (A_2)	A_2 B_1 48.52	A_2B_2 50.0

By studying main effect of sex and methods of teaching separately it was noticed that there was no sex difference, and no different methods of teaching. Now let us examine their interaction effect. From the table 6.7 it is seen that the mean of male physical science teachers is greater than the female physical science teachers. But in case of biological science, mean of female biological science teachers is great than the mean of male biological science teachers. Hence, it is clear that two independent variables, viz., sex and methods of teaching work interdependently on dependent variable attitude towards science subject.

H_{05} : There is no significant interaction effect between sex and area on the attitude of prospective science teachers towards science.

Table 6.8

Dichotmoised Means of Sex and Area

Area (c)	*Urban*	*Rural*
Sex (A)	(C_1)	(C_2)
Male (A_1)	A_1C_1 48.07	A_1C_2 46.87
Female (A_2)	A_2C_1 49.39	A_2C_2 48.07

From table 6.8 it is further observed that the means of urban teachers are greater than the means of rural teachers in both the sexes. Secondly, the means of female teachers are greater than the means of male teachers at both the levels of area. Hence there is no scope for interaction.

The obtained 'F' value of interaction effect of sex and area is 3.63 as seen in table 6.3. This value does not reach the table value of 'F' at 0.05 level as it is 3.91 with df. 1 and 184.

Hence, H_{05} is accepted and inferred that there is no significant interaction effect between sex and area on attitude towards science. Hence, it is concluded that sex and area do not interact with each other on dependent variable attitude towards science subject. But they work independently and run in same direction on attitude towards science subject.

H_{06} : There is no significant Interaction effect between methods of teaching and area on attitude of prospective science teachers towards science subject.

Table 6.9
Dischotomised Means of Methods of Teaching and Area

Area (C) Method of teaching (B)	*Urban* (C_1)	*Rural* (C_2)
Physical Science (B_1)	B_1C_1 49.24	B_1C_2 49.17
Biological Science (B_2)	B_2C_1 48.12	B_2C_2 47.82

The obtained 'F' value of interaction effect of area and methods of teaching as seen in table 6.3 is 0.12. This value is much below the table value of 'F' at 0.05 level. Hence H_{06} is accepted:

It is observed from table 6.9 that the mean of urban teachers are greater than the means of rural teachers in both methods of teaching. Secondly, the means of physical science teachers are greater than the means of biological science teachers at both t he levels of area.

Hence, it is inferred that there is no significant interaction between methods of teaching and area on attitude of prospective science teachers towards science subject. Methods of teaching and area do not interact with each other but function independently in the same direction.

H_{07} : There is no significant interaction effect among sex, methods of teaching and area on attitude of prospective science teachers towards science subject.

The obtained 'F' value of interaction effect among sex, methods of teaching and area is 0.11 as shown in table 6.3. This value is much below and does not reach the table value of 'F' at 0.05 level with df 1 and 184. Hence, H_{07} is accepted and inferred that there is no significant interaction among the variables, viz. sex, methods of teaching and area on attitude of prospective science teachers towards science.

It is further observed from table 6.2 that the means of physical science teachers are greater than the means of biological science teachers in both the levels of area and in both sexes. Secondly the mens of urban teachers are greater than the means of rural teachers in both physical science and biological science groups and in both sexes. Thirdly, the means of female teachers are greater than the means of male teachers at both the levels of area and methods of teaching.

Hence, it is inferred that the interaction among sex, methods of teaching and area is no significant. Therefore, it is observed that all the three variables function independently and leave no combined interaction effect on attitude towards science.

SCIENTIFIC APTITUDE AND ATTITUDE TOWARDS SCIENCE SUBJECT

Hypotheses

Hyptheses No. 1,2 and 4 remain same as given in introduction para 6.1.0

H_{03} : There is no significant main effect of scientific aptitude on attitude towards science subject.

H_{05} : There is no significant interaction effect between sex and scientific aptitude on attitude towards science subject.

H_{06} : There is no significant interaction effect between methods of teaching and scientific aptitude on attitude towards science subject.H_{07} There is no significant interaction effect among sex, method of teaching and scientific aptitude on attitude towards science subject.

Sample and Strategy

Sample, strategy and analysis remained the same as discussed previously in study 1. The primary data like number of observations in whcih cell, their sum, and their means are presented in table 6.10. The summary of ANOVA was prepared using the primary statistical data is furnished in table 6.11.

Table 6.10

N, Σ X and $\overline{X}$ of eight groups formed on the basis of two Levels of the Three Independent Variables Sex, Methods, of Teaching and Scientific Aptitude on Scores of Dependent Variable, Attitude Towards Science Subject.

Scientific Aptitude (C)	*Male (A_1)*		*Female (A_2)*	
	Physical Science (B_1)	*Biological Science (B_2)*	*Physical Science (B_1)*	*Biological Science (B_2)*
	A_1 B_1 C_1	A_1 B_2 C_1	A_2 B_1 C_1	A_2 B_2 C_1
High (C_1)				
N	24	24	34	34
Σ X	1144	1077	1178	1225
$\overline{X}$	47.66	44.87	49.08	51.04
	A_1 B_1 C_2	A_1 B_2 C_2	A_2 B_1 C_2	A_2 B_2 C_1
High (C2)				
N	24	24	24	24
Σ X	1251	1119	1151	1175
$\overline{X}$	52.12	46.62	47.95	48.95

Discussion

H_{01}, H_{02} and H_{04} are remained same as discussed previously in 6.2.1 under area and attitude towards science subject.

H_{03} : There is no significant main effect of scientific aptitude on attitude towards science subject.

The obtained 'F' value of scientific aptitude as observed from table 6.12 is 1.41. This value is below the table value of 'F' at 0.05 level of significance with df 1 and 184. Hence H_{03} is accepted.

Table 6.11
Summary of Analysis of Variance of Three Independent Variables, Sex, Methods of Teaching and Scientific Aptitude on Dependent Variable Attitude Towards Science Subject.

Source	*Sum-SQR*	*D.F.*	*Mean-Sum-SQR*	*F-Value*	*Remark*
A	99.15625	1	99.15625	1.48200	N.S.
B	85.32291	1	85.32291	1.27524	N.S.
C	26.98958	1	26.98958	0.40339	N.S.
AXB	379.71875	1	379.71875	5.67531	X
AXC	266.01041	1	266.01041	3.97581	X
BXC	40.34375	1	40.34375	0.60298	N.S.
AXBXC	9.19793	1	9.19793	0.13747	N.S.
ERROR	%12310.91699	184	9.19793	0.13747	N.S.

A = Sex
B = Methods of teaching
C = Scientific aptitude
with df 1 and 184 'F' Value at 0.05 = 3.91
with df 1 and 184 'F' Value at 0.01 = 6.81

X Significant
XX Highly significant
N.S. Not significant

Table 6.12
Level Wise Means of Scientific Aptitude

Scientific Aptitide(C)	*Mean*	*M.D.*
High (C_1)	48.91	0.75
Low (C_2)	48.16	

It is further observed from the table 6.12 that the apparent mean difference between high scientific aptitude group. and low scientific aptitude group is 0.75 this is very insignificant. Hence, it is inferred that there is no significant main effect of scientific aptitude on attitude of science teachers.

H_{05}: There is no significant interaction effect between sex and scientific aptitude on attitude towards science subject.

It is observed from table 6.11 that the obtained 'F' value of the interaction effect between sex and scientific aptitude is 3.97. This is significant at the table value of 'F' at 0 05 level. Hence, H_{05} is rejected o.05 level of significance.

Table 6.13
Dichotomised Mens of Sex and Scientific Aptitude

Scientific aptitude (C) *Sex (A)*	*High (C_1)*	*Low (C_2)*
Male (A_1)	A_1C_1 46.27	A_1C_2 49.37
Female (A_2)	A_2C_2 50.06	A_2C_2 48.45

To verify it further it is observed that from table 6.13 that the means of female teachers at both levels of scientific aptitude are greater than the means of male teachers, Again viewing from scientific aptitude angle. The means of male teachers is lesser than female at high level scientific aptitude. But at low level scientific aptitude the mean of male teachers is greater than the female teachers. Hence, it is inferred that there is interaction between sex and scientific aptitude and they pull in opposite direction on attitude towards science.

H_{06} : There is no significant interaction effect between methods of teaching and scientific aptitude on attitude towards science subject.

By studying the main effect of methods of teaching and scientific aptitude separately. Is was noticed that there is no difference in physical science and biological science methods of teaching and high level and low level of scientific aptitude 'F' value of interaction effect of the Paris of methods of teaching and scientific aptitude is 0.6. This value is below the table value of 'F' at 0.01 level of significance with df 1 and 184. Therefore this value is considered insignificant and hence the hypothesis H_{06} is accepted.

Table 6.14
Dichotomised Means of Methods of Teaching and Scientific Aptitude

Scientific aptitude (C) *Methods of teaching (B)*	*High(C_1)*	*Low (C_2)*
Physical Science (B_1)	B_1C_1 50.04	B_1C_2 48.37
Biological Science (B_2)	B_2C_1 47.95	B_2C_2 47.79

To clarify it the means in table 6.14 are examined. It is observed that the means of physical science teachers a high level and low level scientific aptitude are greater than the means of Biological science teachers. The means of high level scientific aptitude group science teachers are greater than the means of low level scientific aptitude groups in both physical science and biological sciences. Hence, there is no interaction. Therefore, it is inferred that both independent variable, viz methods of teaching and scientific aptitude do not interact with each other. It means they pull in same direction on attitude towards science subject.

H_{07} : There is no significant interaction effect of sex, methods of teaching and scientific aptitude on attitude towards science subject.

The obtained 'F' value of interaction among sex methods of teaching and scientific aptitude is 0.13. This value is much below the table value of 'F' at 0.05 level with of 1 and 184. Therefore this value is considered quite insignificant. Hence, H_{07} is accepted.

To clarity this the means of two levels of three variables are presented in table 6.10. It is observed that the means of male physical science teachers are greater than the male biological science teachers at both the levels scientific aptitude groups. Secondly, female biological means are greater than the female physical science at both the levels of scientific aptitude. The means of male biological science high level, and female biological science high level groups are lower than their counter parts. However this difference is not significant. Hence it is inferred that sex, methods of teaching, and scientific apititude function independently and leave no combined interaction effect on attitude towards science subject.

Study 3

SES and Attitude Towards Science

Hypotheses

Hypotheses No.1, 2 and 4 remain the same as given in introduction para 6.1.

H_{03}: There is no significant main effect of SES on attitude towards science subject.

H_{05} : There is no significant interaction effect between sex and SES on attitude towards science subject.

H_{06} : There is no significant interaction effect between methods of teaching and SES on attitude towards science subject.

H_{07} : There is no significant interaction effect among sex, methods of teaching and SES on attitude towards science subject.

Sample and Strategy

Sample, Strategy and analysis remain the same as discussed previously. The primary data like number of observations in each cell, their sum, and their means are presented in table 6.15. The summary of ANOVA was prepared using primary statistical data is furnished in table 6.16.

Table 6.15

N, ΣX and $\overline{X}$ of the Eight Groups Formed on the Basis of Two Levels of Three Independent Variables Sex, Methods of Teaching and SES on the Dependent Variable Attitude Towards Science Subject.

SES (C)	*Male (A_1)*		*Female (A_2)*	
	Physical Science (B_1)	*Biological Science (B_2)*	*Physical Science (B_1)*	*Biological Science (B_2)*
	A_1 B_1 C_1	A_1 B_2 C_1	A_2 B_1 C_1	A_2 B_2 C_1
High (C_1)				
N	24	24	24	24
ΣX	1193	1069	1165	1195
$\overline{X}$	49.78	44.54	48.54	49.79
	A_1 B_1 C_2	A_1 B_2 C_2	A_2 B_1 C_2	A_2 B_2 C_1
Low (C_2)				
N	24	24	24	24
ΣX	1202	1127	1164	1205
$\overline{X}$	50.08	46.95	48.50	50.20

Discussions

H_{01}, H_{02} and H_{04} are discussed previously in 6.2.1 area and attitude towards science subject.

H_{03}: There is no significant main effect of SES on attitude towards science subject.

Table 6.16
Summary of Analysis of Variance of the three Variables Sex, Methods of Teaching and as on Attitude Towards Science.

Source	*Sum-SQR*	*D.F.*	*Mean-Sum-SQR*	*F-Value*	*Remark*
A	99.15625	1	99.15625	1.45035	N.S
B	85.32291	1	85.32291	1.24801	N.S
C	17.48958	1	17.48958	0.25582	N.S
AxB	379.71875	1	379.71875	5.55410	X.X
AxC	8.36542	1	8.38542	0.12265	N.S
BxC	31.71875	1	31.71875	0.46395	N.S
AxBxC	16.28125	1	16.28125	0.23814	N.S
Error	%12579. 5830	184	68.36730	1.00000	

A Sex
B Methods of Teaching
C SES
X Significant
XX Highly Significant
N.S Not Significant

Table 6.17
Level-wise Means of SES

SES (C)	*Mean*	*Mean Difference*
High (C_1)	18.24	0.60
Low (C_2)	48.84	

The obtained 'F' value as main effect of SES as seem in table 6.16 is 0.25. This value is much below the table value of 'F' at 0.05 level Hence, H_{03} is accepted and further inferred that there is no significant main effect of SES on attitude scores.

To test the hypothesis the means of high level SES and low level SES groups are examined in table 6.17. The apparent mean difference between high SES group and low SES group is 0.6 . The value is insignificant. Hence. It is further inferred that there is no difference in the attitude of high level SES group and low level SES group of science teachers towards science subject.

H_{05}: There is no significant interaction effect between sex and SES on attitude towards science subject.

It is observed from table 6.18 that the means of both male and female teachers at high level SES are lesser than the means at low level SES group. Secondly, the means of female teachers are greater than the male teachers at both the levels of SES. Hence, it appears that there is no scope for interaction effect.

Table 6.18

Dichotomised Means of Sex and SES

SEX (A)	*SES* High (C1)	Low (C2)
Male (A1)	A_1C_1 47.31	A_1C_2 48.33
Female (A_2)	A_2C_1 49.16	A_2C_2 49.35

It is further clarified from table 6.18 that the obtained 'F' value of interaction effect is only 0.12, which does not reach up to 0.05 level of significance with df 1 and 184. Hence H_{05} is accepted. So it is inferred that both independent variables, viz. sex and SES function independently without interacting with each other on attitude towards science. It means, they pull in the same direction.

H_{06} : There is no significant interaction effect between methods of teaching and SES on attitude towards science subject.

Table 6.19

Dichotomised Means of Methods of Teaching and SES

Method of Teaching (B)	*SES* High (C_1)	Low (C_2)
Physical Science (B_1)	B_1C_1 49.31	B_1C_2 49.40
Biological Science (B_2)	B_2C_1 47.16	B_2C_2 48.58

It is observed from table 6.19 that the means of physical science teachers at both levels of SES are greater than the means of biological science teachers. Secondly, the means of low level SES group are greater than the means of the high level group. Hence, it is clear indication that there is no interaction at all.

It is further clarified from table 6.16 that the obtained 'F' value of interaction is 0.46 which does not reach up to the table value of 'F' at 0.05 level of significance with df 1 and 184. Thus, H_{06} is accepted. It is inferred that both the independent variables, methods of teaching and SES function independently without interacting with each other on attitude towards science. It means, they pull in the same direction on attitude towards science.

H_{07} : There is no significant interaction effect among sex, methods of teaching and SES on attitude towards science subject.

From table 6.15 it is observed that the means of male physical science at both the levels. Thirdly, the means of female physical science at both the levels. Thirdly, the means of low level SES group are greater than the means of high level SES group in both sexes and methods of teaching. So, there is no possibility for interaction.

For clarification, on looking into table 6.16 it is concluded that the obtained 'F' value of the interaction among three independent variables is only 0.23 which does not reach up to the table value of 'F' at 0.05 level of significance with df 1 and 184. This value is insignificant. It shows that there is no interaction. Thereby the H_{07} is accepted. It is inferred that all three variables function independently without interacting with one another on attitude towards science. It means they pull in the same direction.

Study 4

Self-sufficiency Vs. Dependency and Attitude Towards Science

Hypotheses

Hypotheses No. 1, 2 and 4 remained same as given in introduction para 6.1.0

H_{03} : There is no significant main effect of self-sufficiency Vs. dependency on attitude towards science subject.

H_{05} : There is no significant interaction effect between sex and self-sufficiency Vs. dependency on attitude towards science.

H_{06} : There is no significant interaction effect between methods of teaching and self-sufficiency Vs. dependency on attitude towards science subject.

H_{07} : There is no significant interaction effect among sex, methods of teaching and self-sufficiency Vs. dependency on attitudes towards science subject.

Sample and Strategy

Sample, strategy and analysis remained the same as discussed previously in study 1. The primary data like number of observations in each cell, their sum and their means are presented in table 6.20. The summary of ANOVA was prepared using primacy statistical data and is furnished in table 6.21.

Table 6.20

Σ X and $\overline{X}$ of the Eight Groups Formed on the Basis of Two Levels of Sex, Methods of Teaching and Self Sufficiency Vs. Dependency on the Scores of Dependent Variables Attitude Towards Science Subject

Self Sufficiency vs. Dependency (c)	*SEX (A)* Male (A_1)		Female (A_2)	
	Physical Science (B_1)	*Biological Science (B_2)*	*Physical Science (B_1)*	*Biological Science (B_2)*
	A_1 B_1 C_1	A_1 B_2 C_1	A_2 B_1 C_1	A_2 B_2 C_1
High (C1)				
N	24	24	24	24
Σ X	1192	1130	1185	1136
$\overline{X}$	49.66	47.08	49.37	47.33
	A_1 B_1 C_2	A_1 B_2 C_2	A_2 B_1 C_2	A_2 B_2 C_1
Low (c2)				
N	24	24	24	24
Σ X	1203	1066	1144	1130
$\overline{X}$	50.12	44.41	47.66	47.01

Discussions

H_{01}, H_{02} and H_{04} are remained same as discussed previously in 6.2.1 under area and attitude towards science subject.

H_{03} : There is no significant main effect of self-sufficiency Vs. dependency on attitude towards science subject.

It is observed from table 6.21 that the obtained 'F' value of main effect of self-sufficiency Vs. dependency is 0.09. This value is below the table value of 'F' at 0.01 level of significance with df 1 and 184. Hence, H_{03} is accepted.

It is further clarified from table 6.22 that the mean differences of self sufficient group and dependent group teachers are examined. The apparent mean difference of 0.35 is insignificant. Hence, it is inferred that there is no significant main effect of self-sufficiency vs. dependency personality trait on attitude towards science.

H_{05} : There is no significant interaction effect between sex and self-sufficiency Vs. dependency on attitude towards science subject.

Table 6.21

Summary of Analysis of Variance of Three Variables, Sex, Methods of Teaching and Self-sufficiency Vs. Dependency on Attitude Towards Science

Source	*Sum-SQR*	*D.F.*	*Mean-Sum-SQR*	*F-Value*	*Remark*
A	99.15625	1	99.15625	1.49679	N.S.
B	85.32291	1	85.32291	1.28797	N.S.
C	5.98958	1	5.98958	0.09041	N.S.
AXB	379.71875	1	379.71875	5.73196	X
AXC	102.13541	1	102.13541	1.54176	N.S.
BXC	16.05209	1	16.05209	0.69517	N.S.
AXBXC	310.03125	1	310.03125	4.68000	X
ERROR	%12189.25000	184	66.24593	1.00000	

A = Sex
B = Methods of Teaching
C = Self sufficiency Vs. Dependency
X = Significant at 0.05 level
N.S. = Not Significant
F value at 0.05 level with d.f. 1 and 104 = 3.91
F value at 0.01 level with d.f. 1 and 104 = 6.81

It is observed from table 6.21 that the obtained 'F' value of interaction of sex and self-sufficiency Vs. dependency is 1.54. This value does not reach up to the table value of 'F' at 0.05 level of significance with df 1 and 184. Thus, the H_{05} is accepted.

Table 6.22
Level-wise Means of Self-sufficiency Vs. Dependency

Self sufficiency Vs. Dependency (C)	*Mean*	*Mean Difference*
Self Sufficient group (C_1)	48.36	0.35
Dependent Group (C_2)	48.71	

Table 6.23
Dichotomised Means of Sex and Self-sufficiency Vs. Dependency

SEX (A)	*Self sufficiency Vs. dependency (C)*	
	High (C_1)	*Low* (C_2)
Male (A_1)	A_1C_1 40.30	A_1C_2 47.27
Female (A_2)	A_2C_1 48.95	A_2C_2 49.30

It is further clarified from table 6.23 that the means of female teachers at both levels of self -sufficiency Vs dependency are greater than the means of male teachers . Secondly the means of self-sufficient group is greater in male teachers. But in case of female the mean of dependent group is greater than self sufficient group. However, this difference is very insignificant.

Therefore it is inferred that both the independent variables sex and self-sufficiency Vs. dependency function independently with out interaction with each other, It means they pull in same direction on attitude towards science.

H_{06} : There is no significant interaction effect between methods of teaching and self- sufficiency Vs. dependency on attitude towards science subject.

It is observed from table 6.24 that the means of self sufficiency group in both high P.S. and low B.S are greater than the means of dependency group. Secondly, the means of physical science teachers are greater than the means of biological science teachers at both the levels. Hence. There is no scope for interaction.

It is further clarified from table 6.21 that the obtained 'F' value of interaction is 0.69 which does not reach up to the table of 'F' at 0.05 level of significance with df 1 and 184. Thus, the H_{O6} is accepted. Therefore, it is inferred that both the independent variables function independently without interaction with each other on attitude towards science. It means, methods of teaching and self - sufficiency Vs. dependency pull in the same direction.

Table 6.24

Dichotomised Means of Methods of Teaching and Self-Sufficiency Vs Dependency

Method of teaching (B)	*Self sufficiency Vs. dependency (C)*	
	Self sufficiency (C_1)	*dependency* (C_2)
Physical Science (B_1)	B_1C_1 49.52	B_1C_2 48.89
Biological Science (B_1)	B_2C_1 48.20	B_2C_2 47.54

H_{07}: There is no significant interaction effect among sex, methods of teaching and self - sufficiency Vs dependency on attitude towards science subject.

From table 6.20 it is observed that the means of physical science teachers are greater than the means of biological science teachers at both levels of self - sufficiency Vs dependency and in both sexes. Secondly, the means of self sufficient female teachers are greater than the means of dependent group teachers in both the methods. But in case of male, it differs in their counter parts. Thirdly the means of self sufficient group are greater than dependent group in all cases except in male biological science teacher. Hence, there is scope for interaction.

For clarification on looking into table 6.21 it is seen that the obtained 'F' value of the interaction effect among three independent variables is 4.6 . This value is above the table value of 'F' at 0.35 level. It shows that there is interaction among sex, methods of teaching and self-sufficiency Vs. dependency. Therefore, the H_{O7} is rejected and further inferred that three variables function interdependently with one another on attitude towards science. It means, they pull in the opposite direction.

Study 5

Dominance Vs. Submissiveness and Attitude Towards Science

Hypotheses

Hypotheses No. 1, 2 and 4 remained same as discussed in introduction para 6.1.0

H_{O3} : There is no significant main effect of dominance Vs. submissiveness on attitude towards science subject.

H_{O5} : Thee is no significant interaction effect between se and dominance Vs. submissiveness on attitude towards science subject.

H_{O6} : There is no significant interaction effect between methods of teaching and dominance Vs. submissiveness on attitude towards science subject.

H_{O7} : There is no significant interaction effect among sex, methods of teaching and dominance Vs. submissiveness on attitude towards science subject.

Sample and Strategy

Sample, strategy and analysis remained same as discussed earlier in study 1. The primary data like number of observations in each cell. their sum and their means are presented in table 6.25. The summery of ANOVA was prepared using primary statistical data is being furnished in table 6.26.

Discussions

H_{O1}, H_{O2}, H_{O4} are discussed previously in 6.2.1 under area and attitude towards science subject.

H_{O3} : There is no significant main effect of dominance Vs. submissiveness on attitude towards science subject.

It is observed from table 6.26 that the obtained 'F'value of the main effect of dominance Vs. submissiveness is 0.47, which does not reach the table value of 'F' at 0.05 level of significance with df 1 and 192. This value is not significant, hence, H_{O3} is accepted.

Table 6.25

N. ΣX and $\bar{X}$ of eight groups formed on the basis of two levels of sex, methods of teaching and dominance Vs. submissiveness on the scores of dependent variable attitude towards science subject.

Dominance Vs. Submissiveness (c)	*SEX (A)* *Male (A_1)*		*Female (A_2)*	
	Physical Science (B_1)	*Biological Science (B_2)*	*Physical Science (B_1)*	*Biological Science (B_2)*
	A_1 B_1 C_1	A_1 B_2 C_1	A_2 B_1 C_1	A_2 B_2 C_1
Dominance (C1)				
N	24	24	24	24
ΣX	1098	1135	1183	1206
$\bar{X}$	45.75	47.29	49.29	50.25
	A_1 B_1 C_2	A_1 B_2 C_2	A_2 B_1 C_2	A_2 B_2 C_1
Submissiveness (C_2)				
N	24	24	24	24
ΣX	1297	1061	1146	1194
$\bar{X}$	54.04	44.20	47.75	49.79

Table 6.26

Summary of Analysis of Variance of three variables, sex, methods of teaching and dominance Vs. submissiveness on attitude towards science subject.

Source	*Sum-SQR*	*D.F.*	*Mean-Sum-SQR*	*F-Value*	*Remark*
A	99.15625	1	99,15625	1.56167	N.S
B	85.32291	1	85.32291	1.34380	N.S
C	30.07292	1	30.07292	0.47364	N.S
AxB	379.71875	1	379.71875	5.98042	XX
AxC	157.71875	1	157.71875	2.48401	N.S
BxC	320.34375	1	320.34375	5.04529	X
AxBxC	426.48959	1	462.48959	7,28403	XX
ERROR	%11682.83301	184	63.49366	1.00000	

X Significant at 0.05 level
XX Significant at 0.01 level
N.S Not Significant
F value at 0.05 level with d.f. 1 and 184 : 3.91
F value at 0.01 level with d.f. 1 and 184 : 6.81

Table 6.27
Level-wise means of dominance Vs. submissiveness

Dominance Vs. submissiveness (C_1)	*Mean*	*Mean Difference*
Dominance (C_2)	48.14	
Submissiveness	48.93	0.79

It is further observed from table 6.27 that the mean difference between dominance Vs. submissiveness levels is 0.79 which is very negligible. So, it is concluded that there is no difference in the attitude of dominance Vs. submissiveness groups of teachers towards science subject.

H_{O5} : There is no significant interaction effect between sex and dominance Vs. submissiveness on attitude towards science subject.

Table 6.28
Dichotomised means of sex and dominance Vs. submissiveness

SEX (A)	*Domiance Vs. Submissiveness (C)* (C_1)	(C_2)
Male (A_1)	$A_1 C$ 46.52	$A_1 C_2$ 48.12
Female (A_2)	$A_2 C_1$ 48.70	$A_2 C_2$ 48.75

It is observed from table 6.28 the means of female teachers are greater than the means of male teachers in both dominant group and submissive groups. The means of submissive group are greater than the means of dominant group in both the sexes. Hence, there is no scope for interaction.

It is further clarified from table 6.26 that the obtained 'F' value of interaction effect of sex and dominance Vs. submissiveness is 2.48. This value is below the table value of 'F' at 0.05 level of significance with the d.f. 1 and 184. Hence, H_{05} is accepted at 0.05 level. It is further concluded that sex and dominance Vs. submissiveness function independently and they pull in the same direction.

H_{06} : There is no significant interaction effect between methods of teaching and dominance Vs. submissiveness on attitude towards science subject.

Table 6.29
Dichotomised means of methods, of teaching and dominance Vs. submissiveness

	Method of teaching (B)	
Dominance Vs. Submissiveness (C)	*Physical Science (B_1)*	*Biological Science (B_2)*
Dominance (C_1)	B_1C_1 47.52	B_2C_1 48.77
Submissiveness (C_2)	B_1C_2 50.89	B_2C_2 46.97

It is observed from table 6.29 that the mean of female biological science teachers is greater than the mean of physical science teachers at submissiveness level. But the mean of male submissive teachers is greater than the male dominate group. Hence, there is scope for interaction.

It is further observed from table 6.29 that the obtained 'F' value is 5.04. Hence, the H_{06} is rejected. Therefore, it is inferred that two variables, viz. Methods of teaching and dominance Vs. submissiveness function interdependently and they pull in the opposite direction.

H_{07} : There is no significant interaction effect of sex, methods of teaching and dominance Vs. submissiveness on attitude towards science subject.

From table 6.25, it is observed that the means of male biological science teachers are greater than the means of male physical science teacher in dominant group and male physical science means an greater than male biology in submissive group. Secondly, the means of female physical science teachers are greater than the means of female biological science teachers at high level and lesser at low level. In case of male physical science dominant group mean is lesser than submissive but in other cases dominant group is greater than other groups. Hence, there is scope for interaction.

For clarification, on looking into the table 6.26, it is seen that the obtained 'F' value of the interaction effect among the three independent variables is seen to be 7.28 which is above the table value of 'F' at 0.01 level of significance. Hence, the H_{07} is rejected. Therefore, it is concluded that the three independent variables, viz, sex, methods of teaching and dominance vs. submissiveness function interdependently and they pull in the opposite direction.

Study 6

Introversion vs. Extroversion and attitude towards science Hypotheses

Hypotheses 1,2 and 4 remained same as discussed in introduction para 6.1.0

H_{03} : There is no significant main effect of introversion Vs. extroversion on attitude towards science subject.

H_{05} : There is no significant interaction effect between se and introversion vs. extroversion on attitude towards science subject.

H_{06} : There is no significant interaction effect between methods of teaching and introversion Vs. extroversion on attitude towards science subject.

H_{07} : There is no significant interaction effect among the variables sex, methods of teaching and introversion Vs. extroversion on attitude towards science subject.

Sample and Strategy

Sample, strategy and analysis remained same as discussed earlier in study 1. The primary data like number of observations in each cell, their sum, and their means are presented in table 6.30. The summary of ANOVA was prepared using primary statistical data is furnished in table 6.31.

Discussions

H_{O1}, H_{O2}, H_{O4} are discussed previously in 6.2.1 under area and attitude towards science subject.

H_{O3} : There is no significant main effect of dominance Vs. submissiveness on attitude towards science subject.

It is observed from table 6.31 that the obtained 'F'value of the main effect of introversion vs. extroversion is 4.4 which is above the table value of 'F' at 0.05 level of significance with df 1 and 184 and below 0.01 level. Hence, the H_{03} is rejected at 0.05 level of significance.

Table 6.30

N, Σ X and $\overline{X}$ of eight groups formed on the basis of two levels of sex, methods of teaching and introversion Vs. extroversion on the scores of attitude towards science subject

Dominance	*SEX (A)*			
Vs.	*Male (A_1)*		*Female (A_2)*	
Submissive	*Physical Science (B_1)*	*Biological Science (B_2)*	*Physical Science (B_1)*	*Biological Science (B_2)*
ness (c)	A_1 B_1 C_1	A_1 B_2 C_1	A_2 B_1 C_1	A_2 B_2 C_1
High (C_1)				
N	24	24	24	24
Σ X	1237	1117	1201	1224
$\overline{X}$	51.54	46.54	50.04	51.00
	A_1 B_1 C_2	A_1 B_2 C_2	A_2 B_1 C_2	A_2 B_2 C_2
Low (C_2)				
N	24	24	24	24
Σ X	1158	1079	1128	1176
$\overline{X}$	48.25	44.95	47.01	49.00

Table 6.31

Summary of analysis of variance of the independent variables sex methods of teaching and introversion Vs. extroversion on attitude towards science subject

Source	*Sum-SQR*	*D.F.*	*Mean-Sum-SQR*	*F-Value*	*Remark*
A	99.15625	1	99.15625	1.47918	N.S
B	85.32291	1	85.32291	1.34380	N.S
C	294.98959	1	294.98959	4.40057	X
AxB	379.71875	1	379.71875	5.98042	X X
AxC	0.13541	1	0.13541	0.00202	N.S
BxC	22.71874	1	22.71874	0.33891	N.S.
AxBxC	1.28126	1	1.28126	0.01911	N.S.
ERROR	%12334.33301	184	67.03442	1.00000	

X Significant

N.S Not Significant

F value at 0.05 level with d.f. 1 and 184 : 3.91

F value at 0.01 level with d.f. 1 and 184 : 6.81

Table 6.32
Level wise means of introversion Vs extroversion

Introversion Vs. Extraversion (c)	*Mean*	*M.D.*
Introvert (C_1)	49.1	1.27
Extrovert (C_2)	47.9	

To examine further the means of two levels of introversion Vs. extroversion are presented in table 6.32. The apparent mean difference which is in favour of introvert teachers is 1.27. Hence, it is concluded that introvert teachers have more favourable attitude towards science subject.

H_{05} : There is no significant introversion effect between sex and introversion Vs. extroversion on attitude towards science subject.

It is observed from 6.33 that the means of introversion group are greater than the mean of extroversion group in both male and female teachers. Secondly, the means of female students is greater than the means of male teachers at both the levels of introversion Vs. extroversion. Hence there is no scope for interaction.

It is further observed from table 6.31 that the obtained 'F' value of introversion Vs. extroversion is 0.02 which does not reach the table value of 'F' at 0.05 level of significance with df 1 and 184. Hence, H_{05} is accepted at 0.05 level. Therefore, it is further concluded that sex and introversion Vs. extroversion function independently on attitude towards science and the two variables pull in the same direction of attitude.

Table 6.33
Dicchotomised mens of sex and introversion Vs. extroversion

Sex (A)	*Introversion Vs. Extroversion (c)*	
	Introversion (C_1)	*Extroversion* (C_2)
Male (A_1)	A_1C_1 48.68	A_1C_2 47.0
Female	A_2C_1 49.52	A_2C_2 49.0

H_{06} : There is no significant introversion effect between methods of teaching and introversion Vs. extroversion on attitude towards science subject.

Table 6.34
Dichotomised means of methods of teaching and introversion Vs. extroversion

	Introversion Vs. Extraversion (c)	
Method of	*High* (C_1)	*Low* (C_2)
teaching (B)		
Physical Science (B_1)	B_1C_1 49.52	B_1C_2 48.89
Biological Science (B_2)	B_2C_1 48.60	B_2C_2 47.06

It is observed from table 6.34 that the means of introversion groups are greater than the means of extroversion groups both methods of teaching. Secondly the means of physical science teachers are greater than the means of biological science teachers at both levels. Hence, there is no scope for interaction.

It is further clarified from table 6.31 that the obtained value of 'F' introversion effect between methods of teaching and introversion Vs. extroversion is 0.33 which is below the table value of 'F' at 0.05 level of significance with df 1 and 184. Hence, the H_{06} is accepted at 0.05 level and it is further concluded that the two variables function independently on attitude towards science and they pull in the same direction.

H_{07} : There is no significant interaction effect among sex, methods of teaching and introversion Vs. extroversion on attitudes towards science subject.

It is observed from table 6.30 the means of male physical science teachers are greater than the male biological science teachers at both the levels. Secondly, the means of female biological science are greater than the female physical science at two levels. Thirdly the means of introverts are greater than the means of the extroverts in both sexes and methods of teaching. Hence, there is no scope for interaction.

It is further concluded from table 6.31 that the obtained value of 'F' of interaction effect among sex, method of teaching and introversion Vs. extroversion is 0.01 which does not reach the table value of 'F' at 0.05 level of significance with df 1 and 184. Hence, H07 is accepted. Therefore it is concluded that the three variables, viz. sex, methods of teaching and introversion Vs. extroversion function independently and they pull in the same direction on attitude towards science subject.

Study 7

Emotional Stability and attitude towards science

Hypotheses

Hypotheses 1,2 and 4 are remained same as discussed in introduction para 6.1.0

H_{03} : There is no significant main effect of emotional stability personality trait on attitude towards science subject.

H_{05} : There is no significant interaction effect between methods of teaching and emotional stability on attitude towards science subject.

H_{06} : There is no significant interaction effect between methods of teaching and emotional stability on attitude towards science subject.

H_{07} : There is no significant interaction effect among the three variables, viz., sex, methods of teaching and emotional stability on attitude towards science subject.

Sample and Strategy

Sample, strategy and analysis remain same as discussed earlier in study 1. The primary data like number of observations in each cell, their sum, and their means are presented in table 6.35. The summary of ANOVA was prepared using primary statistical data is furnished in table 6.36.

Discussion

H_{O1}, H_{O2}, H_{O4} are dsmr sd discussed previously in 6.2.1 under area and attitude towards science subject.

H_{O3} : There is no significant main effect of emotional stability on attitude towards science subject.

Table 6.35

N, Σ X and $\overline{X}$ of the eight groups formed on the basis of two levels of sex, methods of teaching and emotional stability on the scores attitude towards science subject

Dominance Vs. Submissive ness (c)	*SEX (A)*			
	Male (A_1)		*Female (A_2)*	
	Physical Science (B_1)	*Biological Science (B_2)*	*Physical Science (B_1)*	*Biological Science (B_2)*
	A_1 B_1 C_1	A_1 B_2 C_1	A_2 B_1 C_1	A_2 B_2 C_1
High (C_1)				
N	24	24	24	24
ΣX	1209	1128	1168	1209
$\overline{X}$	50.37	47.00	48.56	50.37
	A_1 B_1 C_2	A_1 B_2 C_2	A_2 B_1 C_2	A_2 B_2 C_1
Low (C_2)				
N	24	24	24	24
Σ X	1186	1068	1161	1191
$\overline{X}$	49.41	44.00	48.37	49.62

Table 6.36

Summary of analysis of variance of the independent variables sex methods of teaching and introversion Vs. extroversion on attitude towards science subject

Source	*Sum-SQR*	*D.F.*	*Mean-Sum-SQR*	*F-Value*	*Remark*
A	99.15625	1	99.15625	1.47918	N.S
B	85.32291	1	85.32291	1.34380	N.S
C	60.73958	1	60.73958	0.88984	N.S.
AxB	379.71875	1	379.71875	5.98042	X X
AxC	17.55208	1	17.55208	0.25714	N.S.
BxC	12.01042	1	12.01042	0.17595	N.S.
AxBxC	3.48958	1	3:48958	0.05112	N.S.
Error	%12559.66699	184	68.25906	1.00000	

A Sex
B Methods of Teaching
C Emotion stability
X Significant
N.S Not Significant
F value at 0.05 level with d.f. 1 and 184 : 3.91
F value at 0.01 level with d.f. 1 and 184 : 6.81

It is observed from table 6.37 that the apparent means difference between high level and low level group emotional stability is 1.13. This is may be due to sampling or measurement error.

Table 6.37
Level wise means of emotional stability

Emotional Stability (C)	*Mean*	*M.D.*
High (C_1)	49.10	1.13
Low (C_2)	47.97	

It is further examined from table 6.36 that the obtained value of 'F' of the main effect of emotional stability is 0.88 which does not reach the table value of 'F' at 0.05 level of significance. Hence H03 is accepted at both the levels of significance. Therefore, it is concluded that there is no significant main effect of emotional stability on attitude towards science subject.

H_{05} There is no significant interaction effect of sex and emotional stability on attitude towards science subject.

Table 6.38
Dichotomised means of sex and emotional stability

Sex (A)	*Emotional Stability (C)*	
	High (C_1)	Low (C_2)
Male (A_1)	A_1C_1 48.68	A_1C_2 46.70
Female (A_2)	A_2C_1 49.52	A_2C_2 49.00

It is observed from table 6.38 that the means of female science teachers are greater than the means of male teachers at both the levels of emotional stability. The means of high level emotional stability groups are greater than the means of low level emotional stability groups in both the sexes. Hence, there is no scope for interaction.

It is further observed from table 6.36 that the obtained value of 'F' of the interaction effect between the sex and emotional stability is 0.17 which is below the table value of 'F' at 0.05 level of significance with df 1 and 184. Hence the H_{05} is accepted at 0.05 level. Therefore, it is further concluded that there is no significant interaction effect between sex and emotional stability on attitude towards science. So the two independent variables, viz, sex and emotional stability function independently and they pull in the same direction on attitude towards science subject.

H_{06} : There is no significant interaction effect between methods of teaching and emotional stability.

Table 6.39

Dichotomised means of methods of teaching and emotional stability

Method of teaching (B)	*Emotional Stability (c)* High (C_1)	Low (C_2)
Physical Science (B_1)	B_1C_1 49.52	B_1C_2 48.89
Biological Science (B_2)	B_2C_1 48.68	B_2C_2 47.06

It is observed from table 6.39 that the means of female science teachers are greater than the means of biological at both levels of emotional stability. Secondly, the means of high level emotional stability group are greater than the means of low level emotional stability group in other methods of teaching. Hence, there is no scope for interaction. It is further observed from table 6.36 that the obtained value of 'F' of the interaction effect between the sex and emotional stability is 0.1 which is below the table value of 'F' at 0.05 level of significance with df 1 and 184. Hence, the H_{06} is accepted at both the level of significance. Therefore it is concluded that the interaction effect between methods of teaching and emotional stability is not significant and the two independent variables function independently. Hence, it is concluded that the two variables pull in the same direction on attitude towards the science subject.

H_{07} : There is no significant interaction effect among sex, methods of teaching and emotional stability on attitude towards science subject.

It is observed from earlier hyptheses that sex, methods of teaching and emotional stability do not show any significant effect individually on attitude towards science. But, when three independent variables are taken at a time, there may be interaction on attitude towards science subject.

So, it is observed from table 6.35 that the means of high level emotional stability science teachers are greater than the means of low level group in both the sexes and methods of teaching. Secondly, that the means of male biological science teachers are lesser than the means of male physical science teachers at both the levels. Thirdly, the means of female physical science teachers are greater than the female physical science teachers at both the levels of emotional stability.

Hence, there is no scope for interaction. It is further observed from table 6.36 that the obtained value of 'F' of interaction effect of sex, methods of teaching and emotional stability is 0.05 which is below the table value of 'F' at 0.05 level of significance with df 1 and 184. Hence, the H07 is accepted at 0.05 level. Therefore, it is further concluded that the three variables sex, methods of teaching and emotional stability function independently and pull in the same direction.

Summary, Findings, Discussion and Suggestions

Summary

The modern civilization is scientific civilization. Modern society is increasingly being influenced by the scientific environment. The application of science has become a part and parcel of our daily life. The speed with which science and technology are racing, is very much felt not only by scientists, economists, administrators, but also by the educationists. It is very much reflected on the teaching-learning process too. The training imparted to the prospective teachers goes a long way in moulding the future of the individual children and the society at large. Including positive attitude towards science and scientific interest are the needs of the hour.

Teaching and learning of science is very much emphasized as it develops certain faculties of reasoning and experimentation. As Galilio has rightly said, "the authority of the thousand is not worth the humble reasoning of the single individual". It also trains the individual to observe, to analyze, to test and to generalize.

The report of Education Commission (1964-66) has also laid emphasis on science based education : "There is one thing about which we feel no doubt or hesitation, that is science based education in coherence with Indian culture and values can alone provide the foundation as also the instrument for the nation's progress, security and welfare."

Science as a teaching subject possess various values like other subject. It is included in the curriculum as a teaching subject as it inculcates intellectual values, utilitarian values, moral values, vocational values, cultural values, aesthetic values, etc.

The real significance of science gained momentum from the beginning of the 19th Century and that is why we observe t hat science occupied less important place in school curriculum during the earlier days. The pursuit of science was the hobby of the people with means and leisure or the solitary efforts of some one with scientific talents in those days. But now we live in a scientific world whether we like it or not. Therefore, science is no longer confined to a few devoted persons, but has become a compulsory subject in every system of school education right from the elementary stage.

The study of science is expected to bring behavioural change in the learner which helps to develop his personality. Science gives opportunity for creative thinking and constructive imagination. Further, science is a subject where ideas can be experimented upon and verified. The learner is expected to develop curiosity and concern for truth. Able all it helps in the immediate application to the world around him. It , therefore occupies an unique place in the curriculum and it is made a compulsory subject, and it is a part of the teacher training programme too. The learning, the training and the attitude of teachers very much helpful in inculcating scientific thinking, both in the students and prospective teachers and in the society at large. So, the researcher felt the need to study the attitude of prospective secondary school science teachers towards science subject in relevance to psycho-social factors and decided to work on this problem.

To study the role of psycho-social factors the researcher selected scientific aptitude, SES, self-sufficiency vs. dependency, dominance vs. submissiveness, introversion vs. extroversion and emotional stability, sex area and methods of teaching as independent variables.

After making a detailed study of different techniques of sampling, random cluster sampling technique was found to be the most appropriate technique for the present study. Regarding the size of the sample 500 was found to be appropriate. This sample was collected from five colleges of Education of Krishna and Guntur districts of A.P. The sample gives fair representation of the prospective science teachers of both sexes, coming from rural and urban areas with different SESs and selecting physical science and biological science as one of the methods of teaching.

Selection of the tools needed an intensive study and the following tools were adopted by the researcher.

1. Science Attitude Scale (Avinash Grewal)

2. Scientific Aptitude Scale (AK.P. Sinha & LNK Sinha)
3. Socio Economic Scale (Beena Shah)
4. Self-sufficiency vs. Dependency scale (A.S. Patel)
5. Dominance vs. Submissiveness Scale (A.S. Patel)
6. Introversion vs. Extroversion (A.S. Patel)
7. Emotional Stability (A.S.Patel)

Based on the objectives of the study Null hypotheses were framed and tested statistically.

Observations

The study involves numerous activities at various stages of the work. All these cannot be handled solitary by the researcher, so help was taken from the different people. First the prospective science teachers helped b answering the tests. They were curious to know the purpose. A worthy observation made by the researcher was many of them enjoyed science attitude scale. Comparatively, more time was taken to answer scientific aptitude scale.

The institution authorities were kind enough in extending their full cooperation in providing for smooth administration of the tests.

For the purpose of the analysis the raw data was fed to the computers. The computer personnel helped the researcher with their programmes right from the preparation of frequency distribution table to 2x2x2 factorial design. This is how all played their role in the completion of the work.

Research requires an abundant patience, devotion and pains, however, it becomes a matter of joy and satisfaction when one passes through that process.

Findings

The findings that are drawn from seven studies are divided into two major parts. Part I deals with main effects of different independent variables on dependent variable attitude towards science subject. Part II. deals with interaction effects of different independent variables on dependent variables attitude towards science subject. In all the studies sex and methods of teaching kept common for factorial design. Therefore, the main effect of sex and methods of teaching as well as interaction of the sex and method of teaching are common.

Part I: Main effects of independent variables

a) Effect of sex : The analysis of the attitude scores on the basis of sex as main effect reveals that there is no significant difference in the attitude of male and female prospective science teachers towards science subject.

b) Effect of methods of teaching. The analysis of attitude scores on the basis of methods of teaching as main effect reveals that there is no significant difference in the attitude of prospective physical science and biological science teachers towards science subject.

c) Effect of area : The analysis of attitude scores, on the basis of area as main effect reveals that there is no significant difference in the attitude of urban and rural prospective science teachers towards science subject.

d) Effect of scientific aptitude : The analysis of attitude scores on the basis of scientific aptitude reveals that there is no significant difference in the attitude of high level scientific aptitude group and low level scientific aptitude group of science teachers.

e) Effect of SES : The analysis of attitude scores on the basis of SES reveal that there is no significant main effect of SES on attitude of science teachers towards science subject. So it is concluded that SES does not play any role on possessing of attitude towards science subject.

f) Effect of self-sufficiency to dependency : The analysis of attitude scores on the basis of self-sufficiency vs. dependency personality trait revels that there is no significant difference in the attitude of self-sufficient group and dependency group of science teachers towards science subject.

g) Dominance vs. submissiveness effect : The analysis of attitude scores reveals that there is no significant difference in the attitude of dominant group ad submissiveness group of science teachers towards science subject.

h) Effect of introversion vs. extroversion personality trait : The analysis of attitude scores reveals that there is significant main effect of introversion vs. extroversion on attitude of science teachers towards science subject. Introvert group of science teachers have more favourable attitude than extrovert group towards science subject.

i) Effect of emotional stability : The analysis of attitude scores reveals that there is no significant difference in the attitude of high level emotional stability group and low level emotional stability group of prospective science teachers towards science subject.

Part II. Interaction effects of different independent variables

i) Sex and other independent variables

a) Sex and methods of teaching : Sex and methods of teaching do not play any role independently. But these two independent variables showed their interaction effect on attitude of prospective science teachers towards science subject. Male physical science teachers and female biological science teachers have more favourable attitude than their counter parts.

B) Sex and area : There is no significant interaction effect between sex and area on attitude of prospective science teachers towards science subject.

c) Sex and scientific aptitude : Sex and scientific aptitude do not show their effect independently. But these two independent variables combined they showed their interaction effect. There is significant interaction effect between sex and scientific aptitde on attitude of prospective science teachers towards science subject Male and high level scientific aptitude group of prospective science teachers have more favourable attitude than other group towards science subject.

d) Sex and SES : There is no significant interaction effect between sex and SES on attitude of prospective science teachers towards science subject.

e) Sex and Self-sufficiency vs. dependency : There is no significant interaction effect between sex and self-sufficiency vs. dependency on attitude of prospective science teachers towards science subject.

f) Sex and dominance vs. submissiveness : There is no significant interaction effect between sex and dominance vs. submissiveness on attitude of prospective science teachers towards science subject.

g) Sex and introversion vs. extroversion : There is no significant interaction effect between sex and introversion vs. extroversion on attitude of prospective science teachers towards scien-- subject.

f) Sex and emotional stability : There is no significant interaction effect between sex and dominance vs. submissiveness on attitude of prospective science teachers towards science subject.

g) Sex and introversion vs. extroversion : There is no significant interaction effect between sex and introversion vs. extroversion on attitude of prospective science teachers towards science subject.

h) Sex and emotional stability : There is no significant interaction effect between sex and emotional stability on attitude of prospective science teachers towards science subject.

ii) Methods of teaching and other independent variables

a) Methods of teaching and area : Methods of teaching and area do not show any interaction effect on attitude of prospective science teachers.

b) Methods of teaching and scientific aptitude : There is no significant interaction effect between methods of teaching and scientific aptitude on attitude of prospective science teachers towards science subject.

c) Methods of teaching and SES : There is no significant interaction effect between methods of teaching and SES on attitude of prospective science teachers towards science subject.

d) Methods of teaching and self sufficiency vs. dependency : There is no significant interaction effect between methods of teaching and self sufficiency vs. dependency on attitude of prospective science teachers towards science subject)

e) Methods of teaching and domiance vs. submissiveness : Methods of teaching and dominance vs. submissiveness do not play any role independently on attitude of prospective science teachers. But these two variables interact each they showed their effect. It is found that there is significant interaction effect between methods of teaching and dominance vs. submissiveness on attitude of prospective science teachers towards science subject.

f) Methods of teaching and introversion vs. extroversion : Methods of teaching does not play any role on attitude whereas introversion vs. extroversion personality trait has its effect on attitude towards science subject. But when these two variables interact with each other they do not show any effect. Hence, it is concluded that there is no significant interaction effect between methods of teaching and introversion vs. extroversion personality trait on attitude of prospective science teachers towards science subject.

g) Methods of teaching and emotional stability : There is no significant interaction effect between methods of teaching and emotional stability on attitude of prospective science teachers towards science subject.

iii) Interaction between three independent variables

a) Sex, methods of teaching and area : There is no significant interaction effect among sex, methods of teaching and area on attitude of prospective science teacher towards science subject.
b) Sex, methods of teaching and scientific aptitude : There is no significant interaction effect among sex, methods of teaching and scientific attitude of prospective science teacher towards science subject.
c) Sex, methods of teaching and SES : There is no significant interaction effect among sex, methods of teaching and SES on attitude of prospective science teacher towards science subject.
d) Sex, methods of teaching and self-sufficiency vs. dependency : There is no significant interaction effect among sex, methods of teaching and self-sufficiency vs. dependency on attitude of prospective science teacher towards science subject. Sex, methods of teaching and self-sufficiency Vs. dependency did not show any effect individually on attitude of science teachers. When these three variables are combined, they pull in opposite direction.
e) Sex, methods of teaching and dominance vs. submissiveness : Sex, methods of teaching and dominance vs. submissiveness do not play any role independently on attitude towards science subject. But these three variables interact among one another they played a role. Hence, it is concluded that there is significant interaction effect among sex, methods of teaching and dominance vs. submissiveness on attitude of prospective science teachers towards science subject.

f) Sex, methods of teaching and dominance vs. submissive : There is no significant interaction effect of these variables on attitude of prospective science teachers towards science subject.

g) Sex, methods of teaching and emotional stability : There is no significant interaction effect among sex, methods of teaching and emotional stability on attitude of prospective science teachers towards science subject.

Discussion

It is very happy to know that the prospective science teachers are having favourable attitude towards science subject.

As the teachers are having favourable attitude towards science subject we can expect that this would help the students to learn science subject with great interest. In many of the earlier studies the teachers were having less interest towards science classes. As the results of this study are against to the earlier ones, one can hope that the present perspectives science teachers may bring variety to class room instruction by using different types of teaching learning techniques and by utilizing all the available manual and material resources. The prospective teachers who are having low attitude towards science subject are supposed to enhance their attitude and interest towards science subject by reading scientific material by attending orientation, refresher courses etc., and by participating in conferences, seminars, symposia etc. It is the duty of the science teachers to have a fair attitude towards science subject in order to create a lively and lovely science class rooms and laboratories in our educational institutions. It is also the duty of the teachers to mould the students attitude towards science subject in a favourable manner. The teachers must also posses good attitude towards science subject as these have to develop scientific attitude, scientific aptitude, scientific methods, critical thinking, logical approach, problem solving technique, objective learning and rational evaluation in the students of their subjects.

As per the recommendations four National Policy on Education 1986 the teachers are supposed to develop a questioning mind in the students which requires a through knowledge of science as well as a positive attitude towards the subject.

Unless the science teachers have a favourable attitude towards science subject they may not be a good conditions to fulfil the intellectual aim, utilitarian aim, cultural aim, aesthetic aim, vocational aim, etc. of science teaching. And at the same time they may also fail in achieving the objectives such as knowledge, understanding, application, skills, appreciation and scientific attitude if they lack a right attitude towards science subject. They may also lag behind in enjoying the fruits of science if they have no favourable attitude towards science.

With the above discussion one can very strongly say that the prospective science teachers, of course the in-service science teachers also must posses as well develop a favourable attitude towards science subject. We hope that these prospective teachers may bring life to our science class rooms in the years to come after joining the services as science teachers.

II. It is found that there is no significant difference in t he attitude of male and female prospective science teachers towards science subject. This is in support of the findings of Misra, Gupta and Misra and Harey and Stables and t his is against to the findings of Banu where the male students have more favourable attitude than female students.

From the above conclusions it can be said t hat the sex, when given equal opportunities has no role to play in influencing the attitude of prospective science teachers towards science subject

In general people and educationists say that the male community having good exposure to exhibitions, fairs, museums, zoos, gardens and such other scientific experiences, will posses a good attitude toward science subject. The result of the study contradicts with the above general opinion and puts the female on par with the male. If equal opportunities are given as observed in this study to both the sexes the female teachers will help the children both at work place and at house. As our former prime minister late Pandit Jawaharlal Nehru opined, "if you educate a man you are educating a single individual, if you educate a woman you are educating the entire family". To adhere this opinion we can say that the female teachers must help the children learn science well.

III. The teaching methodology has also no effect on the attitude towards science subject. As the methodology has no effect on the attitude towards science subject the prospective teachers must develop this attitude through independent studies and activities irrespective of their subject they prefer to teach. As biological science and physical science are the main components of science subjects they may be equally promoting the favourable attitude in them unknowingly. The prospective science teachers, irrespective of their teaching method of expected to develop more favourable attitude towards science subject to teach science subjects effectively in their respective classes. Method of teaching should interaction effect only with se and no with any other variables, may be due to influence of sex on methods of teaching.

IV. There is no effect of area on the attitude of prospective science teachers towards science subject when it was taken as third independent variable. It is also not having any interaction effect on attitude towards science when (i) sex (ii) methods of teaching as the other independent variables.

Usually urban prospective science teachers are supposed to posses a high attitude toward science subject as they have more chances of exposure to various types of scientific experiences and good infrastructural facilities in the institutions. But this study states that the exposure to scientific events and good institutional facilities have no bearing to develop a favourable attitude towards science subject.

V. The study has identified no effect of scientific aptitude on the level of attitude towards science subject though the prospective science teachers have different levels of scientific aptitude. There is no interaction effect among scientific aptitude, sex and methods of teaching which are supposed to influence the attitude towards science subject.

Aptitude is a fundamental concept in promoting a favourable attitude towards the subject. Unless one has no interest and aptitude in a subject he may not be in a position to pursue it in a successful way. Contradicting there generalizations this study reveals that the prospective science teachers have a favourable attitude towards science subject irrespective of the level of scientific aptitude that they posses. But when scientific aptitude interacts which sex there is significant difference in the attitude of prospective science teachers.

VI. The socio-economic status has no effect on the attitude of prospective science teachers towards science subject. It is also not having any interaction effect with sex and methods of teaching.

It is a good sign that the socio-economic status has no bearing on the attitude of science teachers towards science subject. If the teachers forget about their socio-economicstatus and think that they are the teachers to build the nation, they will prepare the students with great eminence. There is every possibility of the influence of SES on the teachers attitude and performance which deserves due attention to multiply the negative impact at time and situations.

VII. Self-sufficiency vs. dependency personality trait has no effect on attitude of prospective science teacher. The prospective teachers whether they are self-sufficient or dependent they possess the favourable attitude towards science subject. But it interacts with sex and methods of teaching at a time there is significant difference in the attitude of prospective science teachers.

VIII. In this study it is found that there is no significant difference in the attitude of prospective science teachers having the personality traits dominance vs. submissiveness. It is a little but surprise to know that the dominate prospective science teachers with aggressiveness, stuffieness and competitiveness are having the same level of attitude towards science subject with submissive teachers having mildness, easiness, closileness and accomodativeness as their characteristics. But this trait of personality interacts with sex and methods of teaching at a time there is significant difference among different groups.

IX. As per the results of the study there is a significant difference in the attitude of introvert and extrovert prospective science teachers towards science subject. The important characteristics of introverts as defined by Carl Yng such as thinking reading, creativeness, constructiveness and alertness might have helped the introvert prospective science teachers to develop a high favourable attitude towards science subject. When compared with the extrovert science teachers having to develop a high favourable attitude towards science subject. When compared with the extrovert science teachers having sociability, courageousness, interest, less thinking ability as their characteristics. As introverts include philosophers, poets, writers, scientists and saints. The results of the present study is in support of the psychological observations.

X. This study reveal that there is no difference in the attitude of prospective science teachers with high level and low level emotional stability towards science subject. As the difference in the levels of maturity and emotional stability are lacking any influence on the attitude towards science it can be condoled that the attitude towards science does not require any emotional stability. The emotional stability may be helping the personality of an individual but is not in any way helping the teachers to upgrade their attitude towards science subject.

In conclusion, it is to be reported that the prospective science teachers are holding a favourable attitude towards science subject which is to be very much appreciated.

Suggestions for further research

This study brings to light some near areas to be studied by the researchers. The areas and variables which are not covered by this study may be put to test to enlighten the other factors associated with the attitude, of prospective science teacher towards science subject. Hence, the researchers may consider the following areas for critical observations:

1. Studies may be taken up in other levels of education to find out the attitude towards science subject.
2. Studies may be conducted by arranging controlled and experimental groups to identify the various Factors that promote favourable attitude towards science subject.
3. Studies may be carried out to identify the role of environmental factors in enhancing or reverting the favourable attitude towards science subject.
4. Studies may be conducted to identify the role of other psychological variables, in influencing the attitude towards science subject.
5. Studies may be carried out to find out the role of achievements or success in science in influencing the attitude towards science subject.
6. Studies may be conducted to identify the influence of teachers, parents, education institutions, libraries, laboratories, mass media, mussres, gardens, zoos, excursions, etc. on attitude towards science.

Bibliography

Adam, G.. (ed) 1962). The Science Master's Book I & II, UNICEF, Paris.

Agarwal, J.C. 1975, Educational Research, Arya Book Depot, New Delhi.

Agarwal K.K. 1986, Manual for Scientific Aptitude Test Battery. National Psychological Corporation, Agra.

Agarwal R.N. 1964. Education and Psychological Measurement. Kalidas Printing Press. Agra.

Allpprt, Gordon, W. 1967. Attitudes Regarding in Attitude Theory and Measurement. University of Illinois. Illinois.

Anderson, L.W. 1985. Attitudes and Their Measurement. The International encyclopedia of education research and studies. Vol. I.

Anderson, J. et al. 1971. Thesis and Assignment Writing. Willey Eastern (P) Ltd. New Delhi

Atkinson, S.K. (ed.) 1970. The Education's Encyclopedia. Englewood Cliff Prentice Hall, Inc., New Jersey.

Bandhyopadhaya, J. 1984. Environment Influence Academic Achievement and Scientific aptitude as determinates of adolescents attitude towards Science. Ph.D. in Psychology.

Banu, D.P. 1986. Secondary School Students Attitude towards Science. Research in science education Vol. XIX.

Barnhart, L.C. (ed.) 1958, Comprehensive Desk Dictionary Vol. II. Doubleday company, Inc. New York

Best, John, W. 1982. Research in science education, 4th ed. Prentice Hall of India (P) Ltd., New Delhi.

Bhaskara Rao, D. 1997 Scientific Attitude. Discovery Publishing House, New Delhi.

Bhaskara Rao, D. 1994 Scientific Aptitude. Ashish Publishing House, New Delhi.

Bhaskara Rao, D. 1989 A Comparative Study of Scientific Attitude, scientific aptitude and achievement in biology at secondary school level, Ph.D. Education O.U. Hyderabad.

Bhaskara Rao, D. 1989. Objectives of Science. Science Promotor. 32.

Bhaskara Rao, Digumarti, 1982, Education for Individual Responsibility, Educational India, 48.

Bhaskara Rao, D. Sundaa Rao, 1988. The Science Teacher has a Definite Role, The Hindu.

Blommers, Paul and Lindquist, F.E. 1965. Elementary Statistical methods. University of London, London

Borg, W.R. Gall, M.D. 1983. Educational Research - An introduction Longman, New York.

Brown R. 1965, Educational Psychology. Free Press. New York.

Brunkhorst, Herbert, K. and Robert E. Yager, 1986. A new rationale for science education. The Education digest.

Buch, M.B. (ed.) 1991 Fourth Survey of Research in Education. Vol. I & II NCERT. New Delhi.

Carlwell, Otis W. and Francis, D. Curtis, 1943. Everyday Science. Ginn and Co., Boston.

Chainulu, C.V. et al. 1988. Methods of Teaching Science, Triveni Publishers, Machilipatnam.

Courts G.S. 1952. Education and American Civilization, Baremma Publications, New York.

Cronbach, Lee. J. 1960. Essentials of Psychological Testing Harper and Brothers. New York.

Crow D. Laster and Crow Alice. 1973 Educational Psychology, Eurasia Publishing House Pvt. Ltd. New Delhi

Das, R.C. 1958 Science Teaching in Schools. Sterling Publishers Pvt. Ltd. New Delhi.

Desai, H.G. 1973 A Survey of Research in Education. Saurashtra University, Rajkot.

Edwards, Allen, L. 1957 Techniques of Attitude Scale Construction. Appleton Century Crafts Inc. New York.

Edwards, Allen L. 1968 Experimental Design in Psychological research. A merind Publishing Co. Pvt. Ltd. New York.

Fowler, H.W. and Fowler, F.G. (ed.) 1968. The Concise Oxford Dictionary of current English, Oxford University Press, 5th ed.

Gage, N.L. 1966. Handbook of research on teaching, Round McNally & Co., Chicago.

Garret, Henry, E. 1979. Statistics in psychology and education. Peffer and Simon Pvt. Ltd. Bombay.

Garret, H.E. and Woodworth, R.S. 1969. Statistics in psychology and Education. Vakils Fefer and Sons Pvt. Ltd. Fifth Edition, Bombay.

Gaynan K. (ed.) 1956. Concise Dictionary of Science. Peter Owners Ltd. , London.

George, A.F. 1966. Statistical Analysis in Psychology and Education. McGraw Hill Book Co. New York.

Ghose, S. 1986. A critical study of scientific attitude and scientific aptitude of the students and some determinants of scientific aptitude unpublished Ph.D. thesis in Education, Kal University.

Giri, B.K. 1976. Measurement of aptitude for the study of Physics of the high school science seniors of the State Bihar with special reference to the students Chota Nagpur Division Ph.D. in Education Rajasthan University.

Glimer, van Hallen, B. 1976. Psychology. Harper and Row Publishers, New York.

Good, C.V. (ed) 1945. Dictionary of Education I. McGraw Hill Book Co. London.

Good C.V. 1959 Dictionary of Education II. edition McGraw Hill Book Co. London.

Good C.V. et al. 1941. Methodology of Educational Research Appleton century Crafts Inc. New York.

Guilford J.P. 1987. Personality. McGraw Hill Publishing Co. Ltd. New Delhi.

Guilford, J.P. 1985. Psychometric methods . Tata McGraw Hill Publishing Co. Ltd. New Delhi.

Haney, Rechard, E. 1984. The development of scientific attitude. The science Teachers, 31.

Harvey, T.J. and Stables, A. 1986. Gender differences in attitudes to science for third year pupils. An argument for single sex teaching groups in mixed groups. Research in Science and Technology Education 4(2).

Hariman, P.L. 1950. Dictionary of Psychology. Wisdom Library, New York.

Hiss, Edwood, D. et al. 1950. Modern Science Teaching, Machmillan Co. New York.

Hird P.H. 1954 The Educational Concepts of Secondary Science teaching.

Hoff, G. 1950. Secondary School Science Teaching. The Blaskiston Company. Toronto.

Jose, K.M. 1987. A comparative study of biology achievement of high average and low science aptitude of secondary school pupils unpublished Ph.D. thesis. University of Calicut, Calicut.

Joseph, E.D. 1976. The teaching of science in Tropical primacy schools. Oxford University Press, London.

Karla, R.M. Innovations in science teaching, Oxford and IBH Publishing Co. New Delhi.

Kohil, V.K. 1984. How to teach science? Vivek Publishers, Ambala.

Marries, Norman R.F. 1964. Psychology in industry. Hoghton Miffilin Co. New York.

Misra, A.M. Gupta, M.B and Mishra, N. 1983. A Study of Attitude towards Learning of Science among Schedule Caste Students. Journal of Education and Psychology.

Patel A.S. and B.P. Lulla 1964. Essentials of Writing Research Report. Centre for Advanced study in Education, Baroda.

Rankow, S.. 1986 Minority Students in Science. Sociology of Education Abstracts. Vol. 22.

Rai, B.C. 1983 Methods of Teaching Science. Prakasan Kendra, Lucknow.

Readers digest Great illustrated Dictionary, 1984. The Readers Digest Association Ltd., London.

Reif, Fredrick. Scientific approaches to science education. Physics Today Vol. XXI.

Report of the Education Commission, 1966. Education and National development. Ministry of India. New Delhi

Robson Colin, 1974. Experiment, Design and Statistics in Psychology. Penguin Education, Second education, Hammonds Worth.

Saunders, H.N. 1959. The Teaching of General Science in Tropical Secondary Schools. Oxford University Press. London.

Saxena A.K. 1985. Attitude towards Physics and Cognitive Preference Style among different groups of science students. Ph. D. Education Rajasthan University.

Schibeci, R.A. 1983. Selecting Appropriate Attitudional Objectives for School Science. Science Education Vol. 67.

Sharma R.C. 1989. Modern Science Teaching. Dhanpat Rai & Sons. Delhi.

Sharfit, M. and Sharif, W.C. 1968. Attitude Ego Involvement and Change. John Wiley and Son Inc. New York

Shrivastava, N.N. 1983. A Study of Scientific Attitude and its Measurement. Indian Educational Review.

Shukla V.C. 1977 Kothari Commission Report. Prakasan Kendra, Lucknow.

S. Kinner, Charles, E. 1968. Essentials of Educational Psychology. Asia Publishing House. Bombay,.

Siddique N.N. and Siddiqui, M.N. 1983 Teaching of Science Today & Tomorrow. Daba House, Delhi

Sidhu, K.S. 1985. Methodology of Research in Education, Sterling Publishers (P) Ltd., New Delhi.

Sundarrayan, S. 1989. Higher Secondary Students Achievement in Biology. Experiments in Education XVII.

Sundararanjan. S. and Rajasekhar, S. 1993. Science Class Room Climate and Interests of Pupils. The progress of education Vol. XIII.

Sujatha Kumari, B. 1987 The Relative Efficiency of Science Aptitude Science Interest and Attitude Towards Science in Predicting Biology Achievement of Secondary School Pupils. unpublished M.Ed. Thesis. University of Calicut.

Shukhia, S.P. et al.1 180 Elements of Educational Research. Allied Publishers (P) Ltd. New Delhi.

Sree Kumar S. 1972 A Comparative Study of Science Interest. Science aptitude and Science Achievement in Science Chief Members and non Members of High School Unpublished M.Ed. Thesis, university of Kerala, Trivandrum.

Telri, E.N. (ed) 1960. Webster's New illustrated dictionary. Book Inc. New York.

The Encyclopedia Britanica 1984. Macropedia vol. 2 Encyclopedia Brtanica Inc. Chicago.

The International Encyclopedia of Education, 1985. Pergamon Press, New York.

The International Encyclopedia of Social Science, 1972 vol. I. Free Press. New York.

Thurston L.L. and Chave, E.T. 1929. The measurement attitude, University of Chicago Press, Chicago.

Thorndike, L.R. and Elizabaeth Hagen, 1957. Measurement and Evaluation in Psychology and Education. Willey astern (P) Ltd. New Delhi.

Travers, R.M. 1964. An Introduction to Educational Research : The Macmillan Co. New York.

Udai Pareekh and Venkateswara Rao, 1974. Handbook of Psychological and Social Instruments. Sahitya Mudranalaya, Ahmedabad.

Vaidya Narendra 1967. Problem Solving in Science. S. Chand & Co. Delhi.

Vaidya, Narendra 1976. The Impact of Science Teaching. Oxford & IBH Publishing Co. New Delhi.

World Survey of Education Vol. III 1971 UNESCO Paris.

Woodwroth R.S. 1990. Psychology, Hanry Hall and Company, New York.

Index